CRICUT AND CROCHET FOR BEGINNERS

2 BOOKS IN 1

The Ultimate Step-by-Step Guide To Start and Mastering Cricut and Crochet With Tips, Tools and Accessories to Create Your Perfect Project Ideas

Rachel Baker

TABLE OF CONTENTS

CRICUT FOR BEGINNERS

The Ultimate Step-by-Step Guide To Start and
Mastering Cricut, Tools and Accessories and Learn
Tips and Tricks to Create Your Perfect Project Ideas

Rachel Baker

1

publisher.

The information herein is offered for informational purposes solely, and is universal as so. The presentation of the information is without contract or any type of guarantee assurance.

The trademarks that are used are without any consent, and the eBook of the trademark is without permission or backing by the trademark owner. All trademarks and brands within this book are for clarifying purposes only and are the owned by the owners themselves, not affiliated with this document.

DISCLAIMER

All erudition contained in this book is given for informational and educational purposes only. The author is not in any way accountable for any results or outcomes that emanate from using this material. Constructive attempts have been made to provide information that is both accurate and effective, but the author is not bound for the accuracy or use/misuse of this information.

FOREWORD

First, I will like to thank you for taking the first step of trusting me and deciding to purchase/read this life-transforming eBook. Thanks for spending your time and resources on this material.

I can assure you of exact results if you will diligently follow the exact blueprint, I lay bare in the information manual you are currently reading. It has transformed lives, and I strongly believe it will equally transform your own life too.

All the information I presented in this Do It Yourself piece is easy to digest and practice.

INTRODUCTION

Want a few cricut thoughts to the cricut cutting device? Cricut private electrical cutters are joining hand crafts and individuals throughout the nation are astonished at the amount of advanced and lovely items they can suddenly create.

The manner a cricut functions is straightforward: simply load a few of many available cartridges to the cutter, choose what colour card stock you'd love to utilize for this specific layout and cut off. Each cartridge has lots of themed layouts - whatever from seasonal layouts to preferred superheroes - and - cricut users may select one or more layouts from every cartridge. The cut out layouts are stuck on...

- Wall hangings

- Scrapbooks

- Image frames

- Custom greeting cards you name it as what is potential using a cricut.

Maybe the absolute most endearing cricut craft thought is a calendar. Another webpage could be made for every month, and every one of those separate pages can be embellished with various layouts. July, for example, will be trimmed using the designs in this independence day seasonal cartridge while february is the most clear option for the love struck seasonal cartridge. The fun does not stop there, however, along with also the mother's day cartridge will be ideal for may while the Easter cartridge is a standard for April. December is unique is cricut-land, also cricut consumers have a lot of collections of layouts such as the joys of the season cartridge along with also the snow friends cartridge to select from.

What would be without scrapbooks to document each and every waking minute of the most prized possessions: our kids? Together with the cricut cutting system, scrapbooks may be customized to each child, and what might be better compared to mom and kid - or dad and kid - to repay together and select which pictures they'd love to decorate their own images with. Cricut also understands that girls and boys are different and this, although the boys probably will not like utilizing the once upon a princess cartridge, they'd go crazy on the batman: the brave and the bold cartridge. Small women, on the other hand, would likely turn their yummy wake up in the robotz cartridge but might love the Disney tinker bell and friends cartridge. You won't ever be at a loss for cricut scrapbooking ideas.

Your cricut design ideas are not only confined to pictures, however, and alphabets will also be available - such as the sesame street font cartridge along with also the ashlyn's alphabet cartridge - them will come in handy when it is time to customize a present. Ideal gifts would comprise images of pets - or possibly vinyl wall-hangings commemorating a special event like this trip abroad - all, needless to say, adorned with bright and beautiful cricut cutouts. Cricut caters to each eventuality, also, here, the produce a critter cartridge along with also the summer at Paris seasonal cartridge will be perfect to match you cricut home decoration.

Birthdays, graduations, Christmas, Hanukkah, bar mitzvahs, baby showers: that the present list is unlimited and this does not even contain those jobs which are completed"just for fun". Cricut has capsules to suit each and every event - and each and every project - which may be considered. Completing a cricut project collectively is also a superb way to get a family to bond, along with the gorgeous things which are created collectively can be cherished for a life.

The Cricut Expression Cutting Machine

The provo craft cricut expression cutting machine is really a huge hit among crafters. It's received a lot of awards and antiques testimonials from several sources. If you're a scrapbooker, teacher, activities director, or anybody else that wants to make paper craft jobs, you are going to want to learn more about the advantages and disadvantages of this cricut expression.

The cricut expression will reduce paper, cardstockvinyl, as well as vellum to shapes, letters, phrases as well as other layouts efficiently. Now you have the choice of employing a 12"x12" cutting mat to get more compact layouts or even the 12"x24" cutting mat to get bigger ones. On the other end of this spectrum, it is possible to cut bits as little as .25", which permits you to consume all these little pieces of paper you have been saving. A variety of lightweight cartridges full of million of designs can be found to expand the Expression's flexibility.

#Cricut Expression vs the Original Cricut

You may have heard concerning the expression's creator, the cricut, also called the'little insect'. The cricut expression utilizes the very same cartridges and knife blades since the first cricut, but permits more versatility. Due to its compact dimensions, the initial cricut is just effective at cutting edge layouts about half of the size of those ones you're able to produce using all the expression. The multiplier additionally has a lot of features not on the first cricut, for example, capability to modify languages and components of dimensions, cut in landscape or portrait view, utilize numerous cuts for thicker fabrics, or produce mirror images employing the other feature. The LCD display is another new feature which lets you see precisely what you'll be cutting until you cut.

The cricut expression has a few disadvantages within the first cricut. The expression is bigger and requires more room on your table or desk. Should you prefer to go to plants or friends' houses to focus on jobs, the plateau is thicker and more awkward to transfer. The expression can be more costly. On the flip side, it enables considerably more flexibility in your layouts. The capacity to reduce larger items is excellent for producing banners or signage and is very helpful to people who must decorate bulletin boards or other large distances.

#Cricut Expression. . .Cutting Edge Technology

In general, that the cricut expression cutting machine is an exciting new solution for crafters. It's particularly nice for those that have arthritis in their hands or whose hands are a bit shaky. Many crafters may find it will not take long to constitute the first price tag of their expression in the sum of money and time that they save from not needing to purchase or cut their layouts. The cost has dropped substantially in the hefty initial retail cost of $499. If you shop carefully, now you can discover the expression for below $300. There's not any computer or high tech understanding required to apply this tricky machine. You can plug it right into any wall socket and plan to begin your job. You'll need to substitute the knife or cutting mat and you might choose to buy extra cartridges to expand your design abilities. It is not a terrible idea to buy the optional instrument kit, possibly, to make the paper a lot easier to lift out of the leading mat. Aside from that, the expression is nearly carefree. As soon as you have a cricut expression cutting machine, then it will become such an essential part of your crafting, so you may wonder how you ever got along without it.

Greatest strategies for selecting the ideal cricut personal electronic cutter

The array of cricut personal electronic cutter machines was made to automate a number of the fiddly crafting jobs. If you have never heard of these before, then keep reading to learn how to choose your house crafts into another level. In case you know of these, you might be asking yourself how to choose which of those cutting machines will be suitable for you. Within the following guide, i'll be assisting you to choose which of those four cricut versions is the very best match for your needs. In the procedure, you are going to observe the advantages and disadvantages of every machine, to assist you in making an educated choice.

The four versions we are going to be studying would be the normal cricut personal electronic cutter, the cricut produce, " the cricut expression along with also the cricut cake.

The simplest model to check at first is your cricut cake. This differs to others, as it's made with one goal in mind. That's, to make professional looking decorations . It may cut shapes out of bread, fondant, gum paste along with other raw materials. It's extremely much like this cricut expression system, but the working components are changed to make them appropriate for food. That means components which have to be washed can be readily eliminated. If you're searching to make edible decorations, then this is the only choice in the scope. This version retails from approximately $270.

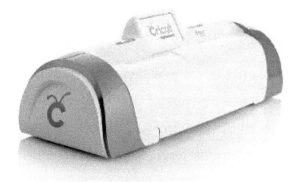

The additional three cricut personal electronic cutter versions are suitable for home printing. They cut from the very same materials, including paper, vinyl, card and vellum. Which version you choose is going to depend upon your budget and requirements.

#budget

The normal cricut personal electronic cutter is the lowest

priced in the scope, costing a minimum of about $100.

Next up is your cricut generate, coming in at $160 and upward.

The surface of the range version is that the cricut expression, that will put you back around $225.

Prerequisites

All versions are compatible with the entire selection of cricut cartridges. This usually means you have an almost infinite supply of cutting edge layouts, since you could always buy more capsules. Therefore there are two important facets in your needs to push your choice. These will be the dimensions of cuts and machine, as well as the assortment of cutting edge choices.

- The conventional personal electronics cutter and make machines are small and mobile. They'll cut contours around approximately 11.5 inches. The produce has a considerably wider assortment of cutting edge purposes.

- The expression is a bigger machine, made to get a permanent spot in a desk or workbench. It'll cut contours around approximately 23.5 inches, and with a large assortment of cutting edge functions.

- By considering these concerns, you ought to have the ability to choose that cricut personal electronic cutter is just the only one for you.

Cricut projects - ideas that may generate income

People really feel the cricut machine is the 1 instrument that's responsible for the conceptualization of these layouts which people see in scrapbooks. In fact, the designs are derived in the brain of the consumer and are made concrete by the cricut cutting device.

In addition, additionally, there are other tools which help make the layouts such as capsules and software applications. The top software tool out there's that the cricut design studio. With this application, you can create and edit your own layouts and also edit current designs which are pre - packed.

Life is great really! People also believe the use of an cricut cutting system is simply restricted to the area of scrapbooking. Not a lot of men and women know of the but there that the cricut machine in addition to the cartridges along with the software tools may be used to get a large number of items. There are a whole lot of cricut projects which you are able to use the cricut cutting system for and just your brain can restrict what you could do.

Greeting cards are excellent cricut projects for anybody to participate in. Together with the layouts which you are able to receive from the cricut cartridge along with the software tools which you have set up, you layout covers which withstand the unconventional. The difficulty that most men and women experience when they attempt to buy greeting cards is that nearly all of the point is they can't locate the plan of this card which they are interested in finding. This may induce anxiety and a great deal of frustration about the purchaser's part. You're a lot better off making your personal greeting cards.

Cricut calendars are another fantastic idea to get a cricut cutting device. A calendar is full of 12 weeks. It is possible to get creative and search for layouts on your cartridge or software which could reflect the entire month that's inside your calendar. If we're at the month of december, then you may search for layouts that fit the mood and feeling of december. Start looking for snowmen, reindeers, and christmas trees. I promise you that you have all of the layouts you will ever desire within your own software or catridge.

Bear in mind, just your imagination can restrict what you do. These cricut projects may be utilized either for private fulfillment or revenue generating functions. Be imaginative with your chosen machine. You never understand what crazy and crazy thoughts can pop in to your mind.

Complex cricut suggestions for the craft project

Cricut private cutters are carrying hand crafts to another new degree. People throughout the nation are astonished at the amazing and advanced cricut thoughts this machine may bring to a project listing. You may create virtually anything amazing and one of a type employing the cricut cartridges.

How does one cricut machine function? It is very straightforward. Simply put in a cricut cartridge to the machine, then choose what colour card stock that you would like to utilize for your individual layout and cut off. Each chance has different themed layouts from seasonal layouts to popular cartoon characters. You are able to pick in the cut designs out to use for decorations, picture frames, picture frames, customized greeting cards, wall hangings, calendars and a lot more.

One of the amazing cricut thoughts you are able to create as the craft is your cricut calendar. Every month can be produced in another page and you may decorate these pages using various layouts. Could not it be wonderful to make your february webpage working with the love struck season cartridge? The easter cartridge will supply you with unlimited layouts to the april page calendar. Your may calendar could be made in the mother's day cartridge. How interesting is it to style your july webpage with trimmings made in the independence day season cartridge? December could be equipped together with all the joys of the season cartridge along with snow friends cartridge. You are able to select for your heart's content.

Another fantastic idea you'll be able to possibly make is your scrapbook. This well-loved craft project is why cricut cutting machine has been devised in the first location. Together with the cricut cutting system, you can customize decorations to your kids, such as mother-daughter or dad and child keepsake. Cricut created capsules which each tiny child would delight in making like the once upon a princess cartridge or even the Disney tinker bell and friends cartridge. Your small super hero will certainly love the batman layout in the batman: the brave and the bold or robotz cartridges. Cricut provides you humungous layouts to select from to the scrapbooking ideas.

The cricut layouts aren't merely lay out thoughts but additionally fonts and alphabets in the sesame street font cartridge along with also the Ashlyn's alphabet cartridge. Use these exciting tools after making your personalized gift like a wall-hanging image frame of having a photograph of a memorable occasion of the receiver of your gift. Embellish your walls hanging with quite cutouts produced by the cricut cutter.

Your cricut thoughts are endless by means of the great machine and also the cricut capsules to match any event and project which it is possible to consider. Creating a cricut project with the entire family is a superb way to spend some time together and producing those gorgeous items can be a terrific experience for everyone to achieve.

Cricut manual for beginners and advanced users

How to utilize the cricut? Basically you add the cartridge,

then set the rubber crucial overlay on the keyboardand turn the device on, then stick a piece of 6 inch paper into the mat which accompanies the device (be certain that you line this up using the tiny arrow onto the mat) press on the"load paper" button and then feed the mat/paper to the machine, then press on the key(s) you to get what you would like to reduce and press on the"cut" button.

If you are a complete novice, you ought to get a scrapbook record with protective sheets (they're fairly affordable, you do not really have to receive the pricey ones). A good colour is generally best, such as black, royal blue . In addition they have patterned/designed ones.

* You should find any paper (12x12, 8x8, 6x6 etc..) not too pricey ($2-4 packs)

* you should find some adhesives to adhere photographs to newspaper (do not use adhesive sticks, so they tend to lift paper and jumble it up) ($.99-3.99)

* get your hands on vases (for example, ribbon, stickers, brads etc) (ranges from $.99-4.99)

* find pencils, archival safe, (such as journaling, be certain they don't bleed, blot) ($2.99-8.99+) sakura jelly rolls, zig millennium, zig memory system, marvy etc..) are fantastic brands & won't ruin paper .

* get your pick dimensions of scrapbook album (6x6, 8x8, 12x12) not pricey ($5.99-19.99) a fantastic dimension to start off would be an 8x8. Approx $7 to this

* receive a newspaper trimmer: to cut extra borders in photographs or reduce paper into a particular dimension ($8.99-19.99)

All these are only the basic items. Do not let shoppers urge choose the very best of you. It happens to most people scrapbookers. We see something adorable that we enjoy but not use it don't want it. Check for earnings. Use coupons in the event that you're able to. Check shops such as the.99 penny stores that also sell rolling sheets for a inexpensive cost & its exactly the exact same thing because the glue you'd locate in michaels for $4-7. Walmart also includes a part of scrapbooking things cheaper than local craft shops (michaels, joanns, hobby lobby etc)

Assess ebay too. There is lots of inexpensive priced things to get.

How To/What to perform precisely:

1. Choose the paper that you would like to utilize. 2. The photograph that you need to add to newspaper. (be certain the

surplus sections of photograph are cut off--to get a nicer appearance utilize your paper trimmer. 3. Utilizing your rolling glue (or"dots") operate it via corners of picture (do not need much only corners & centre). 4. Place picture in newspaper where you wish to. 5. Put any embellishment you might need to decorate it. (this component enables you to be as imaginative as you would like to be.) 6. Journal whatever nice/fun to keep in mind from anything occur or proceeded in that picture. 7. In case you have anything such as brochures, ticket stub or anything, then set them. Make webpages look nicer also.

With countless possibilities using cricut software

The official cricut applications, also called cricut design studio, is a form of software especially designed to create cutting pictures simpler. Using an easy thumb drive apparatus (USB), then you'll have the instantaneous benefit of producing all the layouts which you need that may be cut employing a cricut device. This is just the fastest and handiest link which you may ever need for the your pc and cricut.

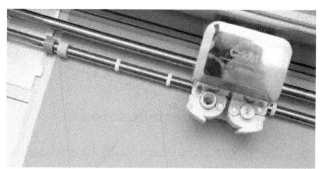

With the support of this Cricut program, you'll have the

ability to produce many designs for any project which you are thinking about. You'll have the advantage of welding, resizing, reshaping, blending as well as twisting pictures of your selection. These attributes alone can provide you more independence and flexibility which you have ever believed possible. On top of that, you don't have to be a genius or a specialist to have the ability to accomplish and make your crafts crafts.

Cricut design studio supposed to provide all craftspeople innumerable advantages. Among those advantages is how the app was pre-loaded with each and every cartridge available for your cricut cutters. This means about a million of distinct designs and patterns which you could use since it's or combine with each other to make a more lovely, distinctive and lavish cutting layouts. Consider the infinite possibilities it's possible to invent, the million of layouts you'll be able to develop. It is possible to also do mixes with your pals.

Now, you might have qualms about getting your self this program since you may consider the approaching new patterns which are going to be available later on. Disregard this notion! Among the most important and funniest advantages of cricut applications is that after you've bought via their official site, you simply must check for newest updates once every so often. When there's a brand new upgraded routine, you do not need to purchase another program to have a hold of this, you just only update your present software and you are all set. The thing which you need to recall here is that irrespective of the amount of designs which you produce, these will just be trimmed and created with the capsules which you have available. However, you don't need to be worried because the cricut will ask you to fit the compulsory cartridge which you need to utilize for your self-improvement routines.

Just imagine the number of jobs which you're able to be in a position to perform with cricut applications. As stated previously, you do not have to be an authority in digital imaging to use this program. This is very fantastic news for novices who hesitate to utilize unique kinds of crafting applications. The very best thing about this particular toll is that it has an interface that's totally user friendly. You are able to easily get the hang of it before you know it, you'll be hooked on utilize the applications with each combination you can consider. There are almost no limitations to what you may design and produce with this program. So go ahead, try cricut and then begin your own scrapbooking adventure.

CHAPTER ONE
WHAT IS CRICUT?

C ricut is your brand-name of a merchandise array of home die-cutting machines (or cutting plotters) utilized for scrapbooking and assorted endeavors, created from Provo Craft & Novelty, Inc. (also known as"Provo Craft") of Spanish Fork, Utah. The machines have been used for cutting paper, felt, vinyl, cloth and other items like fondant. Cricut is one of many digital die cutters utilized by newspaper crafters, card makers and scrapbookers.

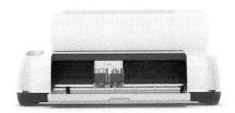

Models

The initial cricut machine needed cutting coasters of 6 × 12 inches, the much bigger cricut explorer simply lets mats of 12 × 12 and 12 × 24. The biggest machine will create letters by a half inch to 23½ inches . The cricut along with cricut explorer air two demand mats and blades that may be corrected to cut various varieties of paper, vinyl and other sheet solutions. The cricut private paper cutter functions as a paper filler predicated upon cutting edge parameters programmed into the system, and looks like a printer. Cricut cake creates stylized edible fondants cut various shapes in fondant sheets, also can be used by chefs at the groundwork and ornamentation of all cakes.

Present Models

These versions are now compatible with the present cricut design space program.

Cricut research 1

The explore it's really a wired die cutting tool which can cut an assortment of materials from paper to cloth and much more. Be aware: there's a wireless bluetooth adapter available for sale individually. This machine just had one instrument slot machine compared with other currently supported versions which have 2.

Cricut research air

The explore air is really a wireless die cutting machine that may cut many different materials from paper to cloth and much more. This system is basically the same as its next iteration, aside from the home and slower cutting skills.

Cricut research air two

The explore air two is small refresh of this research air line that included three colours (mint blue, rose anna, giffin lilac) in addition to a quick mode to reduce back vinyl, iron-on, and card inventory at"around 2x speeds"

Cricut maker

The cricut maker is really a brand new lineup on august 20, 2017, made to cut heavier materials like balsa wood, basswood, non-bonded cloth, leather, and sensed.

The maker is your sole cricut machine which supports the usage of a blade for cutting edge cloth directly, and also a steering wheel with varying pressure to score heavier papers compared to the initial scoring stylus.

Legacy machines

First cricut

The first cricut has a 6" x 12" cutting mat and graphics can be trimmed in a range between 1" into 5 1/2" tall. The first cricut can be used with original cricut cartridges. The first cricut doesn't have the capability to cut many distinct kinds of materials the newer cricut machines may. But, cricut does create a deep cut blade & housing that may allow initial cricut owners to reduce stuff around 1.55mm thick, for example bark, chipboard, and postage materials. The first cricut can also be compatible with all the cricut design craft room.

Cricut expression

The cricut expression® provides several benefits over the former version. To begin with, it permits users to reduce shapes and fonts in a variety between 1/4" into 231/2", and has a 12" x 12" cutting edge with flexible slides so users no longer will need to trim down their media to 6" x 12". It cuts a larger assortment of substances, such as vellum, cloth, chipboard, vinyl, and thin foils. Additionally, it offers an lcd display to preview the job, and contains features such amount and auto-fill. Even a"paper saver" style and selection of portrait or landscape orientation also have been included. The fundamental version has two capsules within the buy, plantin schoolbook along with accent essentials.

Cricut picture

This system was completely unique because it had an hp 97 ink jet printer built to it that it may either cut and publish pictures. This system had a revamped touch screen interface, also has been extremely big and heavy. The device had a very short lifetime of nearly 1 year.

Cricut expression two

The cricut length 2 includes an upgraded exterior from that the cricut expression. It includes a 12" x 12" cutting mat. This system doesn't have the keyboard the first cricut along with also the cricut expression consumed. Rather it sports a brand new full-color lcd touch display. The lcd touch screen shows the computer keyboard on the display and lets you view where your pictures are going to be on the mat before cutting. Additionally, it has the newest characteristic of independent picture sizing and picture turning directly over the lcd display.

Cricut mini

The cricut mini is a tiny private electronic cutting machine. Unlike another cricut machines it simply works using a pc, it cannot cut pictures standing independently. You need to utilize cricut craft room layout computer software. The cricut mini includes over 500 pictures which are automatically unlocked once you join your cricut using all the cricut craft room design applications or your cricut gypsy apparatus. The machine will not have a cartridge jack that's compatible with cricut cartridges except that the cricut picture capsules. The cricut mini also offers a exceptional mat dimensions of 8.5" x 12". The cricut mini may cut pictures in a selection of 1/4" into 11 1/2". Even the cricut mini relied solely on utilizing cricut craft room, a computer software which no longer works. Of the legacy cricut machines, the mini is the only person which is outdated and not usable at all. As no recourse has been supplied to the clients who had bought cartridges for that system, provo-craft has become the focus of several complaints for clients who had been left without a recourse with this sudden pressured'sun-setting' of this machine.

Cartridges

Designs are produced from components saved on capsules . Each cartridge includes a computer keyboard overlay and education booklet. The plastic computer keyboard overlay suggests key collections for this chance only. Nevertheless lately provo craft has published a"universal overlay" which can be used with cartridges released after august 1, 2013. The objective of the universal overlay would be to simplify the practice of clipping by simply needing to learn 1 keyboard overlay rather than being required to find out the overlay for every individual cartridge. Designs could be cut on a pc using all the cricut design studio applications, on a USB attached gypsy device, or could be directly inputted onto the cricut device employing the computer keyboard overlay. There are two forms of cartridges font and shape. Each cartridge has many different creative attributes which could allow for countless distinct cuts from only 1 cartridge. There are over 275 capsules which can be found (separately from the system), including shapes and fonts, together with new ones added each month. When some cartridges are standard in articles, cricut includes licensing arrangements including Disney, pixar, nickelodeon, sesame street, dc comics along with hello kitty. The cricut lineup includes a variety of costs, but the capsules are synonymous, but not all choices on a cartridge might be accessible with the more compact machines. All cartridges work just with cricut applications, needs to be registered to one user to be used and can't be offered or given away. A cartridge bought for a stop machine is very likely to turn into useless in the point that the machine is stopped. Cricut reserves the right to stop support for a number of versions of the applications at any moment, which may make some capsules instantly obsolete.

What Can Be A Cricut Machine?

The Cricut Explore Air is really a die-cutting system (aka craft plotter or cutting edge system). You can Consider it such as a printer; you also make an image or layout in your own personal computer and Then ship it to your device. Except that Rather than printing your layout, the Cricut machine cuts out of whatever substance you desire! The cricut research air can reduce paper, vinyl, cloth, craft foam, decal paper, faux leather, and longer !

In reality, if you would like to utilize a cricut just like a printer, then it may do this also! There's an attachment slot on your system and you're able to load a mark in there after which possess the cricut"draw" the layout for you. It is ideal for obtaining a stunning handwritten look if your design is not all that good.

The cricut explore air may reduce stuff around 12″ broad and includes a little cutting blade mounted within the system. When you are prepared to cut out something, you load the stuff on a sticky mat and then load the mat to your machine. The mat holds the material in place while the cricut blade moves over the substance and cuts . If it finishes, then you unload the mat in the machine, then peel off your project the mat, and then you are all set to move!

Using a cricut system, the options are infinite! All you want is a cricut system, design space, some thing to reduce, along with your creativity!

What could I do with a cricut machine?

There are a lot of things you can perform using a cricut device! There is no way that I could list all of the possibilities, however, here are a couple popular kinds of jobs to provide you a good concept about exactly what the machine could perform.

· cut out interesting shapes and letters to get cartoon

· make habit, handmade cards for any specific event (here is an illustration)

· layout a onesie or some t-shirt (here is an illustration)

· create a leather necklace

· create buntings and other party decorations

· make your own stencils for painting (here is an illustration)

· create a plastic decal for your vehicle window

· tag material on your cabinet, or in a playroom

· make monogram cushions

· make your own christmas decorations (here is an illustration)

· address an envelope

· decorate a mugcup, or tumbler (here is an illustration)

· etch glass at house (here is an illustration)

· make your own wall stickers

· create a painted wooden signal

· create your own window

· cut appliqués or quilt squares

· produce stickers to get a rack mixer

...and plenty of different jobs which are too many to list!

Do It Yourself Using A Cricut Cutter

The cricut cutter is not for everybody. It's not right for the man or woman who's just a casual crafter. It doesn't make any difference if you're a beginner or an advanced crafter it's for the man or woman who's seriously interested in paper crafting. It's a sizable

investment if you don't want to keep busy in document crafting. You sometimes can come across a cutter produce for about $100 in the event that you appear online. This cost can occasionally create the cricut cutter overly pricey for all. As you think about all of the decals, pre-packaged bling, pre-cut letters, numbers, and shapes many scrapbook fans discover the more dedicated scrappers find it eventually cover itself. It's possible to make personalized invitations, gift tags and christmas cards, and then pack and sell them to recover the cost of this cricut. It's by provo craft plus they have a good standing in workmanship, and their products are frequently known to be quite durable, together with replacement components available if desired.

with your own cricut cutter it is a lot less difficult to cut through just about any type or feel of paper. You may also create your own paper, so allow it to dry completely, and then media with your iron (no steam). You are able to use your paper to make real one of a kind cards or scrapbooks and among your kind antiques. Things nobody else has or may understand how to replicate regardless of how hard they try. This will permit your layouts to make original scrapbooks employing a number of shades and textures which may not be replicated.

Experiment together with your cricut cutter. Create new

form and color combinations to permit something distinctive and unforgettable to be found. Shhhhhh... Here's a key tip: following your letter or number or form was trimmed together with your cricut cutter, gently hold the newspaper and choose a tiny rigid craft paint brush, then dip in to future floor wax, also paint the newspaper in which you want the feel to be odd. Let it dry to a plastic plate. Now you can do this a couple times or until you're pleased with the outcome. The newspaper changes feel. Cricut cutter machines have been exceptionally flexible, simple to use, and imaginative enough to be utilized for almost any paper craft project.

A cricut cutter can produce pictures which are "to more than 5" tall. Easy to change capsules are utilized to include customized characters, intriguing boundaries, festive shapes, trendy phrases all made by you to represent your private content of a webpage. Chipboard shouldn't be used or you may hurt the blades. You ought to keep tabs on the sharpness of the blade so that you may have a replacement if necessary. Heavier caliber of cardstock may also result in blades to dull faster. This usually means you'll have the chance to purchase the less expensive paper or cardstock.

- Cricut cartridges sale - the way to save huge on cricut cartridges

- A cricut cartridges purchase is similar to a birthday and christmas morning to most cricut users including novices, beginners or innovative masters.

What Is The Very Best Form Of Cartridge Purchase?

One sale that must not be overlooked is one which features variety. The chance sale which simply can not be passed is one which supplies a huge array of cartridges, like themes and fonts.

For example, by purchasing a couple versatile cartridges such as the beyond birthdays cartridge, alphalicous cartridge and also among those pick disney cartridges, developing a customized card or scrapbook is an absolute breeze. These cartridges offer you extreme flexibility, together with an amazing font, images for special events and some of those much-loved disney personalities to boot up.

The point is a cricut cartridges sale may be the ideal chance to expand a set and in doing this, expand a design that is creative.

Revenue are an ideal time to find the most bang from this dollar. Cartridges, as precious as they are, can certainly accumulate. By taking complete benefit of a circuit breaker purchase, these brand new cartridges are going to be well worth every cent, particularly after making countless names, tags and scrapbook pages.

Cricut wedding undertaking

Here are some fantastic cricut project ideas for creating fantastic homemade greeting cards. This project is for a marriage. It's ideal for giving to a person as a congratulations card to their wedding parties.

Beneath is a listing of items you'll need.

O cardstock: snowy

O patterned paper: purple, pink

O buttons: purple love hearts

O photos of the bride and groom

O pink ribbon

O glue

Directions:

1. Cut a wonderful thick square box. Utilizing graphically speaking orange and cartridge patterned paper, then press shift and reduce on one 4".

2. Cut the name block. Employing the pink cardstock, cut on one 4". Repeat cut employing the purple newspaper.

3. Cut laptop background. Employing the pink patterned paper, then press shift and reduce on one 4".

4. Stick the photos of the groom and bride on the card.

5. Adhere to pink love hearts round the picture of the bridge

and groom.

6. Connect the pink ribbon into a bow then attach the bow on the card.

7. Insert the text such as:"congratulations sarah and richard in your wedding from jean and paul along with loved ones! Xxx"

This need to choose between half an hour and twenty five moments depending how experienced you're using a cricut device. This cricut project thought is really depending on the creative understanding of novices so this isn't a professional cricut job.

Please notice you'll also want:

Recall you may always try various notions you do not have to follow along with the project tutorial step in which you could always alter the color scheme a bit and change the dimensions of this card .

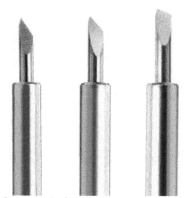

Great Luck with your job!

The base camp cricut chance is a ribbon cartridge that's fantastic for scrapbooks, stationary and people all-important commemorations honoring our servicemen and servicewomen. With decoration and assorted designs that match a broad selection of jobs, cricut novices and experts should take a peek at what the base camp cricut cartridge has to offer you.

7 Base Camp Cricut Cartridge Tips

1. The base camp chance is about endurance, endurance and flexibility. With these qualities in your mind, users may benefit as much or as little as they need from this innovative instrument. The crucial thing is to make the most of this cartridge offers, so understanding it from top to base.

2. The ribbon is a simple alphabet, with this extraneous glitz within different fonts. It consistently contains numerals 0-9 and many symbols that are common. Using a straightforward and traditional font like this one, consumers may use it in almost any capacity. Use it to get the two formal jobs and ones which are only for pleasure.

3. Together with the ribbon, in addition, there are a number of graphic phrases. These include: " I miss you, kiss kiss hug hug, i(heart)u4evr, thank you, happy birthday, usa, as well as the, to and from. These heartfelt sentiments may be used to

get a huge array of motives, but since the title would imply, each one these graphical phrases may be utilized to enjoying thoughts and prayers to our troops.

4. Another tip would be to utilize the cartridge to make personalized cards, invitations, and thank you notes as well as present tags for nearest and dearest. By employing the images, in addition to the innovative attributes, making such things is a breeze.

5. Another suggestion is to utilize all that's featured within this innovative tool to make handmade picture frames for the closest friends and nearest and dearest. Pick out a couple of your favourite cartridge phrases such as"kiss kiss hug hug" and"i(heart)u4evr" and then set them along the borders of the framework.

6. The base camp cartridge includes several creative alternatives that may be used to include shapes and much more to a paper crafts. These attributes include: label, dog tag,

appeal, shadow, rectangle and much more.

7. With these innovative attributes, users can quickly create their dog tags and allure. To get gift-wrapping and celebrations, users may also use those attributes to create place cards, name tags and prefer tags.

With so much to provide, it's no surprise that individuals everywhere are visiting that the cricut base camp cartridge to the flexible and functional tool it is. Produce something private with all the base camp cricut chance and also these 7 helpful hints.

Cricut cartridge - remembrance of holidays past

This season with the assistance of all cricut cartridge, start a brand new holiday tradition by collecting your zest to get a nostalgic family record. Provo craft cricut capsules give a hand in assisting you to create designer fashion scrapbook pages.

The scrapbook craze swept america in the civil war into the 1880s fueled from the vibrant pictures and folds up scenes of vacation collectibles that recipients desired to maintain and exhibit. The scrapbooks functioned as cherished reminders as the decades pass.

Beautiful illustrated postcards in the 19th century have been thrown off in temples for safekeeping. Historians follow holiday greeting cards into 18th century schoolboys who wrote intricate letters for their parents to demonstrate their improvement created in penmanship.

In the olden times, scrapbookers painstakingly pasted the attractively decorated calendars and cards into records using an alternative made from bread and water. Antique cards are still appeal now. An collection of early 1900s published postcards exemplifies memories brought to life and maintained in history.

Nowadays, using cricut cartridge names like calligraphy collection and jasmine capsules, it is possible to provide that old world design feel to your present art endeavors. Contain sourcing and paper clippings for an individual touch.

Seven Easy Steps To Completing The Fantastic Scrapbook Page:

- Select a motif.

- Co-ordinate newspapers.

- Crop photographs.

- Mat pictures.

- Page design.

- Create name and diary.

Insert memorabilia and antiques.

* Die cut letters produce a fast name or going for almost any design.

* pictures can be obsolete or garnished with chalks or

emphasized with gel pens.

* a shadow effect may be only created by clipping out the exact same letter in two distinct colours.

* the contours can then be overlapped, permitting the underside color to show through.

* use leftover bits for cutting letters out to lessen waste.

For finishing a particular scrapbook, pick a set of photos or just one big photo to your front cover. On account of this huge cricut cartridge catalog, the novice scrapbooker might be readily overwhelmed.

The great news is that modern scrapbooking is now a communal previous moment. Finding inspiration from other scrappers and hints on that cricut cartridges will probably work great for you is an easy click away.

Opposites bring, storybook, and wild card chance are simply a couple of the wonderful choices available to help you in your trip for remembrance of vacations past.

What exactly does cricut cartridges need to offer you?

There are all sorts of cricut capsules that anybody can utilize. These cartridges work in several types and are designed to take care of an assortment of distinct products. They are also able to be simple to handle at a cricut apparatus. The characteristics that include these capsules are remarkable and must be utilised to make some fine styles that anybody can handle.

All these cricut capsules are all created using the exact same bodily layouts. This is done to make it a lot easier for an individual to load and then remove a cartridge out of a cricut apparatus. The crucial thing is to maintain the magnetic characteristics that connect the chance into the apparatus clean and simple to control. This is indeed that the cartridge will keep working and it could.

A cartridge will contain two important points. To begin with, it is going to feature a unique font. This font may relate to a particular theme and may incorporate both upper and lower case items as well as some numbers and special characters.

The cartridge may also incorporate a collection of shapes and images. These can be different by every cartridge. These ought to be viewed to make nice looks which are cut correctly and equally if the cricut machine functions correctly.

The topics that cricut cartridges may include are extremely appealing. These capsules may include things like topics which vary from traditional holiday motifs to ones which deal with specific interests such as flowers, animals, sports and other items. The assortment of cricut capsules that anybody can locate is so enormous it might take some time to list all of the available choices.

each cartridge may also incorporate a great keyboard design that will examine the computer keyboard onto the cricut apparatus. This is utilized to aid with distributing advice on which the particular kind of layout may be. It's designed to keep things recorded carefully and to make sure that data is made to where it is not going to be too much hassle to handle.

A number of those distinctive cartridges may also incorporate items which work with various colours in your mind. Included in these are layouts in which the appearance can match along with specific paper colours. A complete guide may be utilized to indicate that paper things which have to be used carefully. This ought to be handled to maintain things looking as good as they are sometimes.

There are a number of those capsules that may work with particular designs taken for classroom requirements. By way of instance, 1 alternative can use a layout which permits a consumer to produce cutouts of fifty countries. Designs may also be built to cut cursive letters to ensure it is simpler for pupils to understand to operate with specific procedures of writing in school. The layouts can be exceptional but they ought to be assessed carefully.

People should consider how cricut cartridges may operate in several types. These layouts are created to produce some great looks which are created to maintain all sorts of functions working nicely regardless of what types of things one must manage.

Which Are Cricut Machines And Why Are They So Popular?

Cricut machines have altered the world of crafting. These machines are particularly popular with crafters since they're fun, easy to use, and also conserve punctually. If you like to decorate and craft, all these machines are a must have! There are lots of versions of cricut machines in provo craft including the expression, expression two, picture, private cutter, mini, gypsy, produce, cake, cake mini, along with martha stewart crafts edition. There's a die cutting tool which will suit you and your kind crafting.

All these machines will provide you exact die cuts each moment. No longer cutting edge and crafting by hand. This saves an immense quantity of time, and that means that you are able to begin on additional projects you have not had the opportunity to enter. You may work on multiple jobs at precisely the exact same time should you would like. Cricut machines paired together with the countless themed cricut cartridges accessible from provo craft offer you unlimited chances for your creative side.

Cricut machines supplies a huge array of cartridges for almost any event you can consider. The expense of the cartridges vary from $25 to around $60 per year. These capsules have fonts and graphics which could be customized for all of your endeavors. You might even change the textures and colours of your own materials and achieve unique looks with your endeavors utilizing exactly the identical cartridge. In case you have family or friends which likewise craft using cricut machines it's possible to swap or borrow capsules to save cash.

Cricut machines could be bought online or in a craft shop. Obviously, the cost depends upon the version you decide on. Their cost can vary anywhere from $100 to $350 generally. On some occasions, it is possible to discover excellent deals hunting on the internet for revenue or locate a secondhand one. As soon as you discover the model that's ideal for you, then you ought to create a note regarding what tools are included with that. On occasion you'll have to acquire tools along with this equipment for example cutting off mats, spatula, replacement blades, blades, and needless to cutting stuff for your own project.

As you're able to view these machines really are a substantial investment, but may be quite rewarding and enjoyable for a long time to come. Any crafter may gain in the high-tech inventions and professional-looking jobs regardless of if you're a beginner or pro crafter. Amaze your family and friends with your imagination. Make crafting creative and fun again using cricut machines.

Everything you want to know about the cricut personal cutter before purchasing

Before investing your hard earned cash to a die cutting platform, you have to do your own research. There are numerous versions available on the industry and after much thought this is actually the oneI've selected and why.

The cricut personal cutter system made by Provo craft is a wonderful edition for your own scrapbooking tools. There are some distinct cricut personal cutters. The cricut expressions will reduce 12x 24 inch dimension newspapers. The cricut original cuts 6x12 inch newspaper. Even the cricut cutting mat includes a gentle adhesive and retains your paper in position although the cutting edge is done. Every cricut machine includes a cartridge, so the cricut original includes george & basic shapes and it's a basic cartridge, which unites capital alphabet named george along with a choice of shapes. Each cartridge is made up of capsule, a keypad overlay plus a few include the instruction booklet. So as soon as you've got unpacked your new cricut personal cutter you may begin experimenting immediately away. Down the monitor you further extend the performance of your cricut system, together with other cricut capsules. Provocraft is publishing new cricut cartridges annually and they have broad selection of topics, from alphabets, sports, even in the backyard through to Disney characters.

On that the cricut personal cutter it's possible to correct blade thickness, stress and cutting rate. This assists when cutting different substances. Slowing down the cutting edge rate gives a much better outcome with more delicate scrapbooking paper, even whilst using moderate pressure provides a crisper cut scrapbooking cardstock rather than the softest stress setting.

You can cut shapes and letters by adjusting the dimensions dial from 1 to 5 1/2 inch. The sizes available are 1, 1 11/4, 11/22, two, two 1/2, 3, 31/2, 4, 5 41/2551/2.

The capability to load up the scrapbooking paper, then cut a couple of letters, then unload the newspaper and reload to precisely the point you had been around, saves the time and paper.

The cricut cartridge george along with basic shapes includes six innovative capabilities. Signal up, slotted, charm, silhouette, shadow and shadow blackout.

Signal - envision that a picket sign with a letter or form cut

Slotted - oval ring, a slot clip in the very top to thread ribbon or twine

Charm - your letter or shape cut using a ring attached at the top, so you can join the correspondence using a brad for your design

Silhouette - cuts that the outline of your own letter or form. Great for the budget conscious as you're in a position to maintain the adverse cut of your correspondence and use it on a different design.

Shadow - cuts the letters or contours, slightly bigger than ordinary, these can subsequently be utilized behind the standard dimensions correspondence, giving the look of a shadow along with a 3d effect for your name. This attribute is on each one the cricut capsules.

Cricut sampler cricut cartridge - 7 tips you can use now

The cricut sampler cricut cartridge is easily among the most adored capsules in the full collection and together with"cricut sampler cricut cartridge - 7 tips you can use now," users know seven reasons why this inventive tool never gets older.

The finest way to describe this particular cartridge would be by describing others. The cricut sampler chance is comprised of images and graphics from various well-known cartridges. Initially the chance was created as the greatest starter thing and a trailer of sorts for different capsules. But users immediately realized they got the very best of many worlds and may take advantage of the smorgasbord of images.

Cartridges Contained from the Cricut Sampler cartridge

comprise: Makin' the Grade, Walk into My Backyard, New Arrival, Paper Pups, Opposites Attract, Moving Location, Alphalicious, Fabulous Finds, ZooBalloo, and Printing Press.

Cricut Sampler Cricut Cartridge - 7 Tips You Can Use Now

1. See to the sampler as precisely what it really is! As soon as you've got it, don't adhere to one or 2 of your favourite pictures. Rather, try out just a small bit of what, experimentation and determine why provocraft believed that these capsules were significant enough to turn into a sampler.

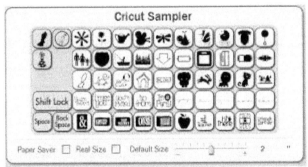

2. Create your own personalized static! This cartridge contains all you want to create a magical and whimsical group of letterheads, envelopes and notes.

3. Produce cards, such as thank you cards, invitations, congratulatory notes, solidarity cards and even cards simply to say hello. With this specific cartridge, it's about just how creative you are using the graphics and images available.

4. Make the most of those phrases. Phrases contain words

such as love, thank you, you are invited, you are the greatest, I miss you, it is a party, joy, limited edition, top secret, number 1 student, number 1,, friends forever, family, love, woof and much more! Add them into pre-made things or produce your own creations.

5. Produce your own gift tags with the assistance of all the particular capabilities. Using the aid of button, then you may make tags and readily distort them together with all the pictures and colors included here.

6. As soon as you've taken advantage of this cricut sampler cricut cartridge, then have a look at another cricut capsules that are showcased in this one. If you're completely satisfied with all the cricut sampler cricut cartridge, then do not bother with others. But in the event that you simply can not get enough of those images, simply have a look at the complete capsules.

7. Make the most of the distinctive capabilities. These attributes may be used to add exceptional effects, such as shadows that add depth to pictures.

The cricut sampler cricut cartridge is exceptional in that, although it's a sampler capsule, it may stand alone on its own as a result of its unbelievable group of pictures. Users may use this cartridge offers and what it does not. Currently, with the assistance of all cricut sampler cricut cartridge.

Cricut Suggestions - Tips About How Best to Make the Most

of Your Own Cricut Machine

The cricut machine was produced for a large number of factors. Now most folks might feel this gadget is exclusively for producing scrapbooks . However, it isn't. The cricut machine may be used for entire lot more of stuff than simply making scrapbooks. If you seem closes in a cricut machine and you also allow your creativity go crazy, you can think of a great deal of great cricut thoughts which could enable you to own a supply of simple or living give your private satisfaction.

As what has been mentioned before, folks associate the usage of a cricut system using only making scrapbooks. Among those excellent cricut ideas which are worth discussing is a cricut machine may also be utilised to make calendars that are fantastic. The cricut machine in addition to the cricut design studio program may be utilized to produce layouts for your own calendar.

One calendar year is constituted of 12 weeks. Please note that every month consistently has a theme for this as being moist, chilly, and there may even be weeks which are noteworthy for a particular occasion. Together with the 2 tools which we just said, it is possible to produce and select layouts which may breathe life into a particular month. Let utilize the entire month of december for instance. December is closely connected with winter and christmas. If we were to make a cricut calendar depending on the month of december, then you will need to pick designs that could mirror this season.

Some fantastic layouts for this month contain reindeers, snowmen, along with santa clause himself. That is so cool would not you say?

In addition to some calendar, the cricut cutting tool may also be utilised to produce your personal gift cards. When you visit malls or to shop that concentrate on selling cards, i'm pretty much certain you'll always be longing for another layout. With the usage of cricut machine together with the attempts from the cricut style studio, then you may produce your gift card with your design and nobody will end you. You're your own boss.

So all these are a few of the most frequent cricut tips which you are able to resort to this will help optimize using your chosen machine. Should you know about several other ways besides that which was just handled, you're free to apply it. It's a free world after all.

Cricut lite cartridges

If you're a craft enthusiast, so you've probably already heard of cricut lite cartridges already. With the rising popularity of garbage reservation, it turns into a remarkably common brand in the world of crafts. When it's for industrial purpose or private hobby, then one is certain to be successful in creating an artistic bit through using devices such as cricut lite cartridges.

All these cartridges are made by the cricut system makers.

The principle intention of creating these instruments is to aid artists to generate more innovative and attractive designs within their various projects. Cricut lite capsules have improved a lot after its launch. To begin with there were just simple white and black cartridges. At the moment, tons of multicolored capsules with vibrant graphics can be found on the industry.

Cricut lite cartridges are extremely manageable. Technically, it's created from plastic which accompanies a thick grip - that can be readily inserted in the cricut system's slotmachine. The device will then browse the things added into it in almost no time.

CRICUT LITE SPECIFICATIONS

As using the cartridge dimensions, it's fine enough to deal with almost any cricut apparatus. Each cartridge comprises many different attractive images - many varieties also consist of different celebration and other intriguing themes. Some cartridges supply a brand new typeface quality which works nicely with upper and lowercase characters.

All cartridges have various images that are related to one another. Examples would be the billionaire cartridge which accompanies a luxury automobile, a hat that is complex, and tube along with the carousel cartridge which has ribbons, jugglers, and other circus material which includes it.

Some cartridges can also arrive with a keypad overlay. This

is a really convenient addition since it reveals exactly what one should get ready for the cartridge. It makes images simple to read and also to place along with a computer keyboard or eliminate them later in the event that you would like.

Cricut lite cartridges arrive in remarkable themes. Each theme has its own own collections of symbols along with a brand new typeface in chosen themes. Some popular topics on the market today contain these:

1. Bloom place - this chance has numerous shrub and blossom designs. It's not difficult to use, without providing issues with your own layers. It includes a coloured instruction card that allows you to observe the qualities and layers of every layout. Bloom cartridge cost is currently at $39.99.

2. Meow place - clearly, it is a motif made from cat images. Such as the bloom collection, it's also readily available for the purchase price of $39.99.

3. Varsity letter series - this collection includes a typeface attribute with group of letters that seem like how it's printed onto a varsity student's coat.

4. Botanicals - this chance allows you observe the beauty of nature via its botanical layouts. Comes with uppercase fonts, so it provides a bit of elegance to your house, scrap books, along with other endeavors. Get your personal botanical chance for $38.95.

5. Cupcake wrappers - this chance is created solely for most

of the cake bakers on the market. It has a bundled 50 cupcake wrappers or picture holders which you may pick from and cut your self to work with to maintain your newly baked cupcakes. You're able to buy cupcake wrappers for cost ranging from $30 - $40.

CONSUMER REVIEWS

In general, consumers locate cricut cartridges helpful due to their scrapbooking and other artwork requirements. With a fantastic choice of themes and shapes, an individual can readily locate a suitable cartridge for virtually any event. Buyers and consumers just whine about the costs that looked somewhat too significant.

Cricut Design Studio - 4 Things You Need to Be Aware of Before Purchasing!

The cricut along with cricut expression house cutting machine have come to be an exciting key for any crafter and trash booker's supply cupboard. Together with the machine's capacity to decrease shapes, letters, and figures at the touch of a button, the cricut is a very simple approach to produce scrapbooking pages, exhibit boards, as well as trendy wall art! The cricut manufacturer has made the system much more intriguing and innovative with all the cricut design studio software. This program takes the cricut system to soaring amounts of imagination. The computer software permits you to hook up your cricut to your house computer and make countless new shapes and designs for the device to reduce.

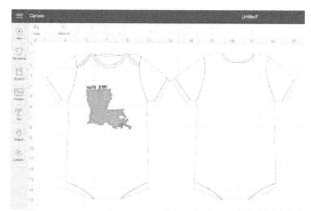

the software comprises a searchable database of each letter, form and amount in the entire cricut cartridge library, so setting tens of thousands of layouts on your palms. And, cricut delivers online upgrades to always increase the library group. Additionally, together with the tools contained, you can get complete control on your own cricut, enabling you to meld (referred welding) letters to a single phrase, and to structure and format objects onto an electronic cutting mat prior to your machine begins its function.

A couple things to keep in mind concerning the cricut design studio software:

1. Although the computer software permits you to see and layout at any cartridge on the market, it's possible to just use the device using all the cartridges you really have. The fantastic thing is that designing distinct things on the pc will provide you a clearer idea about exactly what cartridges you'd like to buy next. Additionally, you may save your layouts for

later usage.

2. Possessing a daily creativity-wise? Want some fresh inspiration? Have a look at the cricut message boards or search the world wide web to look at and get the trendy and imaginative files which additional cricut design studio users've established. This really is a fantastic way to include unique designs to your designs, but additionally to secure fresh and new inspiration.

3. You're able to produce a layout with more than 1 cartridge; you'll simply must have all of the capsules available once you're ready to cutoff.

4. You may still create unique layers to your layouts, such as shadows along with other components. The crucial thing is to make each component on a different layer from the design studio applications to ensure your cricut machine will probably understand to reduce these layers individually and also on the newspaper of your selection.

The cricut design studio software sells for about 6 bucks, and it's a definite must own for any cricut enthusiast. The computer software will loose all your creative thoughts and enlarge the cricut's skills to complete new levels.

Cricut candles - what cricut tote bag works best for the expression machine?

A cricut bag bag is the ideal solution for transporting as well as keeping your cricut machine in your home when you aren't using it. The bags may likewise be employed to keep various accessories such as your capsules and toolkit. The cricut bags generally provide foam cushioning to secure your machine and other pockets for lots of the tools which you may need.

The bigger cricut expression machine is occasionally regarded as the system which shouldn't be carted around. A cricut tote may be utilized to keep the machine in your home, but a lot of croppers prefer to be on the move and visit plants. Bringing their equipment along is essential, therefore you can find now totes which are made large enough to specifically deal with the expression machine. If you're searching for a cricut tote to your own multiplier, ensure the bag is big enough to take care of the larger machine. Tote descriptions especially mention whether the bag is large enough to your expression machine.

One popular storage bag for your expression is a retractable rolling tote. Velcro straps and a solid bottom provide strength and additional reinforcement so the tote can manage the larger expression. The wheels are powerful and the grip makes it effortless to pull alongside you personally. The additional handle makes it feasible to carry them with no usage of these wheels. The interesting part about those bags is that there are various ones out there in trendy colours.

Another option that's readily available for your expression is really a cricut shoulder bag. Picture a massive sport tote and you get a fantastic idea what this bag resembles. It's water proof, and it can be important if transporting an electric appliance. This bag makes carrying out the cricut and additional capsules a breeze since it's extremely roomy. The cushioned and flexible shoulder strap makes the bag comfortable to take. It's also offered in various colors so search about for the colour you want.

A guide to cricut printers and cricut cartridges

Cricut is a renowned brand of server drifting everywhere in the nation. It's an exciting and one of a kind gadget utilized by several people who wish to create creative and excellent projects. As of now, there are 3 unique versions of cricut: the cricut generate machine, luxury cricut expression and needless to say, the foundation version cricut personal electronic cutter machine.

Before improving about that which cricut can give rise to the society, so let us look during its short history. Cricut was initially made by a sizable firm named provo craft that was a little shop. About forty decades back, the organization of provo craft began as a retail shop in the little city of provo, utah. Together with their resourcefulness and imagination, the business eventually expanded after the number of decades. Now, they finally have a total of ten shops with up to 200,000 foot distribution centre.

If you take a close examine the standard cricut machine, so it looks like the visual appeal of a inkjet printer. But it doesn't require a computer to be worked in any way. Even a mean individual may use its purpose as you don't require programming abilities too. Among its advantages include being lightweight. Its blade may also cut thin and thick newspapers that range from 1 inch and 5.5 inches in height.

Cricut only weighs half pounds and that has the power adapter . Additional it's possible to even make it everywhere such as celebration gatherings or event demonstrations because it's a portable item. Using its distinctive and sleek layout, it'll always seem compatible for any crafting office.

As mentioned previously, it could cut to 5.5 inches but that is only one attribute it comprises. It may cut boundaries and names up to eleven inches , therefore, which makes it an ideal match to a newspaper using a measurement of 12x12 inches. Unlike other manufacturers, cricut's key aspect is having the capability to reduce a great deal of stuff. Cricut can also cut a newspaper which has a vast assortment of around 0.5 mm thick. Fortunately, provo craft has supplied additional materials like designer paper pads along with cardstock pads which may be utilized along with cricut cartridges. In reality, these two unique kinds of newspapers are created to have an ideal match with cricut.

Even in the event you ask a lot of users of cricut, then they'd definitely state that cricut digital thermometer is the best one of the top cutters. This is only because cricut cartridges possess a huge selection of choices with respect to styles, fonts and designs, therefore, promoting the maximum degree of imagination without the necessity of a pc.

If you really do not understand using cricut cartridges, they're miniature folds which you put within the cricut for one to place the type of shape, design, font or layout which you would like to cuton. The cartridge even has distinct classes. It comprises: ribbon cartridges, accredited cartridges, form capsules, options capsules and classmate cartridges.

Finally, you're extremely lucky since purchasing a cricut cutter also allows one to get a free cartridge! This totally free cartridge includes some basic shapes which could already provide you the chance to make several shapes and decoration. If not happy, you can purchase additional cricut capsules to add up for your collection. The more chances you have, the greater odds of producing unique artworks.

CHAPTER TWO
USES OF CRICUT MACHINE

Cricut Machine Basics

The cricut machine is leading to a revolution in paper crafting. It's readily portable and operates without being hooked on a computer so that you only pick this up from the handy carrying handle and proceed. But do not allow the advantage fool you, this system isn't a toy. It's capable of producing an unlimited range of letters, shapes, and phrases anything you can imagine. There are no limitations!

The scrapbooking community is mad about the cricut. It's been a celebrity at tens of thousands of"plants" nationally. The testimonials this machine receives from happy clients are remarkable:"beats the contest hands down";"i am happy I bought the cricut along with my entire family is loving it";"teacher's best friend!" ; and"the cricut is fantastic - a fantastic tool to own" are only a couple of the magnificent reviews from amazon buyers.

The cricut machine may generate reductions 1" - 5.5" high and around 11.5" long. There are many cartridges accessible to enlarge the cutting edge choices and stress dials that permit the usage of different varieties of paper.

If you wish to go larger, the most recent addition to this cricut cutting platform is your cricut expression 24" personal electronic cutter. It's two brand new cutting mats that measure 12" x 24" and 12" x 12", that lets you reduce characters out of 0.25" up to an astonishing 23.5"

Six new styles along with a number of new functions provide better customization of reductions, and new configurations permit various components of languages and dimensions. The cricut expression additionally comes with an lcd display that shows just what you are looking for another clip. This significant machine is stuffed with features which make it ideal for your classroom or home enterprise.

Last but surely not least is your cricut produce which combines the durability of their first cricut machine together with the performance of this cricut expression device. The cricut drive machine is smaller just like the first cricut system, but lets cuts out of 0.25" around 11.5" onto a 6" x 12" cutting mat also packs at all the characteristics of this cricut expression such as an eight-way vertical blade, portrait style (to cut off pictures), fit to page style (to reduce the most significant cut potential), auto fill mode (to mass create cuts), center point purpose, and twist function. Additionally, it has a better screen screen and slick design.

Cricut additionally carries all you want to finish your jobs: capsules which contain complete ribbon and contour collections, cutting boards, cutting blades, paper-shaping gear, along with a storage bag.

So What exactly are you waiting for? Obtain a Cricut and make creative!

Which Cricut Machine Should you Purchase?

There are 3 versions of this Cricut system, popular private die cutters produced available by the Provo Craft business. With three great possibilities, it can be hard to choose which to purchase. In the event you start little and purchase the first Personal Electronics Cutter? Or is your Expression model value the additional investment? How can the Generate, the hybrid version now being exclusively offered by Michael's Craft Store, stand against both of the other machines?

In numerous ways, all 3 die cut machines will be precisely the same:

All three versions are cartridge-based.

You can only create cutouts depending upon the capsules you possess. Each cartridge includes a computer keyboard overlay, which can be employed in choosing special cuts. The cartridges aren't machine-specific - they may be utilised in any of those 3 versions.

Fundamental performance of three machines is exactly the exact same.

If you have the personal electronic cutter, then you'll not have any trouble working on the cricut expression or produce (along with vice-versa). Why? The fundamental operation of three die cutters would be exactly the exact same.

Here is a fast rundown of this procedure. After plugging in the chosen cartridge and accompanying computer keyboard overlay and turning to the machine, then you're prepared to begin making die cuts. Materials, like paper or cardstock, are set on a particular cutting edge mat, which is subsequently loaded to the machine using all the press of a switch. With another press on this button, the chosen design is selected. All that is left is to choose"cut". The device does the remainder of the job.

All three cricut machine versions utilize the very same accessories.

It was mentioned that the capsules aren't machine-specific, but in addition, this is true with the majority of the additional accessories. It isn't important which version you have - that the replacement blades, blades, different instruments, like the cricut spatula, and design studio applications, may be utilized with almost any version. The 1 exception is that the cutting mats. The machines take various sizes of their mats, and you need to get one that's compatible with your particular machine.

Now that you understand the way the cricut machines are alike, you're most likely wondering how they're different. They change in many ways:

The dimensions of die cuts made by every machine are distinct.

The personal electronic cutter has the capacity of earning cutouts ranging from 1 inch to 5-1/2 inches in dimension, in half inch increments. The generate can create die cuts that range from 1/4 inch to 11-1/2 inches in dimension, per inch inch increments. The expression provides users the maximum flexibility, making cutouts out of 1/4 inch to 23-1/2 inches in dimension, per quarter inch increments.

They size and weight of these machines change.

The personal electronic cutter and produce are equally small, mobile machines. These versions are great for crafters who prefer to shoot their jobs on the street, and make record layouts and other jobs in class settings. They're also suited for people who don't own a particular place in their house place aside for crafting, since these die cutters are easy to package up and set away between applications. The expression, on the other hand, is considerably heavier and bigger. In case you've got a crafting corner or room, and don't have the worries of transferring it regularly, it is a fantastic option.

The three cricut machine versions have various functions and modes.

There are many distinct modes and purposes. By way of instance, the match to page style will automatically correct the dimensions of this die cut predicated upon the dimensions of this material loaded from the system. The middle point function lets you align with the cutting blade across the middle of this substance, so the cut is created about it. The expression machine gets the most flexibility so much as the access to functions and modes. Next in line would be the produce, and third place belongs to the personal electronic cutter. More info could be found regarding such functions and modes in the system handbooks, which can be found in pdf format on cricut.com.

The cost differs for every version.

The personal electronic cutter is the most inexpensive cricut cutter, having an estimated retail price of $299.99. The generate is $100.00 longer, at $399.99, as well as the rake is $499.99. Please be aware that all 3 machines can be bought at substantial savings. Many retailers operate particular sales or possess a lesser regular cost compared to suggested retail cost. It is a fantastic idea to look around when purchasing your very first cricut machine.

Cricut Machine - Beyond the Scrapbook World

Now most men and women feel the cricut system is only just for producing layouts for scrapbooks. They're extremely wrong when they believe like that. This instrument has helped not just scatter bookers but also manufacturers of cards too. Yes, you heard me when I said present cards. The cricut cutting machine is obviously normally created for the newcomer to sophisticated scrap booker.

This poor boy is accountable for cutting newspapers and other substances into the plan or pattern you would like. The plan or pattern could be gotten with the assistance of tools. There's a really famous software tool on the market known as the cricut circuit design studio that has a great deal of layouts that are jazzy. The very best aspect of the software tool is the fact that it allows you to edit the layout they already possess set up and when new layouts can be found, it is possible to upgrade it. That's really cool! Cartridges also come packed with a great deal of layouts which you might also pick from.

The cricut system as mentioned previously could be utilized to earn cards. I am sure everybody has this horrible experience before of becoming frustrated because the shop that you have didn't have the layout that you desired. It can induce great deal of anxiety facing that reality particularly when the individual who you need to provide the card is quite unique. With the support of this cricut design studio, a pc, along with your cricut cutting machine, then you can think of the layout that you need to your own card and ensure that special someone happy. Besides greeting cards, that instrument may also be utilized to produce hangings for partitions, along with calendars.

If you consider anything else which you could do using all the cricut machine, don't hesitate to apply it. There are not any limitations to what you could do.

If you opt to buy one, and that I truly advocate, you will need to spend $300 or more. If this sounds a little too tight for you, you may always start looking for a fantastic bargain on a cricut machine. Look out for earnings on the regional mall or attempt to buy online from ebay or amazon. But keep in mind you don't necessarily have to choose something that's brand new. If you know somebody which has a second hand device however remains in pristine condition, do it. You have to be a smart buyer and spender in precisely the exact same moment.

Joyful cricut searching!

Marsha brasher was crafting for several decades. She loves the challenge of producing cutting documents, and that she understands what is needed to make handmade crafts having the most complex of designs.

Five Strategies For Buying Secondhand Cricut Machine

If you're thinking about purchasing a secondhand cricut device to conserve cash, you're in luck. Since scrapbookers and paper crafters update and purchase newer versions, you will find lots of older versions which are offered for sale on web sites including eBay and craigslist. Oftentimes, these old versions are in great condition, and may be gotten for a fraction of the price of purchasing brand new, a thrifty deal for those seeking to spend less in these challenging financial times.

But, until you plunk down your hard-won money to get a secondhand cricut machine, then there are a couple of things which you ought to ask the vendor to be certain you are in fact getting a fantastic deal:

1. Does the machine have some known flaws?

Even in case the product description doesn't say the occurrence of flaws, it's a fantastic idea to acquire direct confirmation from the vendor. When asked directly, the vendor might tend to completely disclose the state of the machine.

2. Is the vendor willing to offer a short-term guarantee?

If the vendor asserts the system is in great working condition, learn if they'd be eager to deliver a short-term guarantee, for example you for fourteen days. This demonstrates that the vendor is ready to stand behind their merchandise, and provides you with the chance to test out it to confirm it is really defect-free.

3. What accessories are included with this machine?

Locate out what accessories are all included, and also the status of these accessories. By way of instance, if you obtain the cricut personal electronic cutter brand new in the shop, the subsequent add-ons will be comprised: George cartridge, cutting mat, cutting on blade and housing, cable, usb cable, and documentation. If these things aren't included, the price of replacing them must be factored to a complete cost.

4. What are the delivery costs?

If you're buying a secondhand cricut device from a local vendor, this might not be an issue. But in the event the vendor is sending the machine for you, ensure the transport and handling prices are fair and reasonably priced.

5. Will the vendor supply shipping insurance?

Shipping insurance is relatively cheap, but for a commodity like this that may possibly be broken in the delivery process, it's very good practice to get the carrier assistance, like the post office, ups, and fed ex, supply protection, in the event the merchandise is damaged during transport.

Closing ideas...

Purchasing a secondhand cricut system may be a terrific way to spend less. Provided that you've got an open line of communication with the vendor, and also take the essential actions to secure your investment, then you need to not have any issue.

Affordable Cricut Machines - It's All About eBay

Scrapbooking wasn't a simple procedure back as it was still in its baby years. The true procedure was so dull and meticulous that a little mistake was sufficient to allow you to go mad because you needed to begin all over again. However, with the advent of engineering, things have come to be so much simpler and much more convenient. Now, we've got the cricut machine that is mostly responsible for creating scrapbooking so far simpler than it had been 50 decades back.

For the ones that are somewhat interested in what this gadget is, even the cricut gear is a house die cutting instrument. It's effective at providing patterns to newspaper, cloth, and vinyl sheets. The layouts are saved on cartridges that could be retrieved by means of a computer which has a usb. Now is not that cool? Therefore, if you're really considering getting into the practice of scrapbook creating, the cricut system is a tool which you must possess. But keep in mind, this is sometimes an expensive investment. But if you know where to look then it's possible to acquire affordable cricut machines.

A new cricut gear can cost you more than 300. For the fiscally competent, this is no biggie. However, if you're working at minimum wage and have children to send to college and let you pay, this is sometimes considerable investment. The ideal spot to start looking for affordable cricut machines would be to eBay. Ebay is a website where online vendors meet and market their products. In case you go into http://www.ebay.com and enter cricut machines from this search box, then you'll find a large number of outcomes.

The fantastic thing about ebay is that you have the product

right from the vendor rather than via some channel of supply. That is 1 reason many products being offered on ebay are substantially less costly than what you find about the stores or stalls . Exercise precaution since there may be online vendors who are hacks. 1 fantastic method to inspect the profile of this vendor is to receive their feedback score. A feedback score is the evaluation given by individuals whom the vendor has completed business with. Always target for your 99.9 to 100% feedback score or rating.

On EBay you'll get a blend of used and new economical cricut machines. Bear in mind, new isn't necessarily excellent. There may higher versions of some cricut equipment which isn't so old but can be bought in precisely the exact same cost of a lower end product that's brand new. Proceed for the prior. As a scrapbook manufacturer, it's always clear that you would like to have the highest high quality tool. However, in addition, you ought to be sensible and wise. Enough was said.

Get Creative With All the Cricut Machine - 6 Best Suggestions For The Cricut!

Produce Your Handmade Greeting Cards

Have you gone to a shop to get a greeting card? Additionally, it doesn't matter which kind of card it's birthday, Christmas, Easter or only a favorable thinking of one card to ship off to some long lost buddy, you end up turning it on to observe the purchase price. Generally the cost for only one charge card is around $4.00. That's quite pricey for a very simple card.

Why not rather create your own handmade greeting cards along with your cricut machine and also spare the cash whilst making your personal designs? There are several distinct cartridges for several fun layouts. Get creative, vibrant and motivated while creating these cards.

Produce your very own seasonal decorations

Any holiday or season it's simple to think of a number of your holiday decorations with nothing over cricut machines and scrapbooking supplies. Just envision the Christmas trees, valentine hearts or halloween ghosts you are able to possibly make.

Produce your wall decoration

Why spend hours your self or worse yet selecting a muralist to hand painting your favorite letters onto your own walls. You are able to easily do yourself using vinyl die cuts that can produce the exact same appearance as an expert.

Make your die cut decals

Making your die cut decals are a good way to utilize your cricut device. Die cut decals are a terrific present for young kids who just like to stick them anywhere. You are able to use these to make interesting and vibrant posters, school jobs or even to place in decal books. These decals can be reached in any form possible and are much less expensive as going out and buying them at a craft shop.

Creative scrapbooking ideas

Have a kid or expecting soon? Why don't you produce a scrapbook full of their lifestyle! You are able to begin with the day of the arrival and also keep adding pictures as they grow old. If your kid gets older, it is going to be the ideal present (the narrative of the lifetime).

Party or wedding favors

Use with the tags, bags, boxes and much more cartridge to generate party favor creations simple. You may earn anything out of hats, gifts, bags, banner ads or alternative inventions tailored for your precise celebration or wedding motif and colour.

All these are some tips which you may use to make interesting projects together with your defeatist machine. Learn more about the world wide web to discover even more thoughts. Let your creativity go crazy.

Utilize your cricut machine to generate money scrapbooking

If you're into scrapbooking whatsoever no doubt you've learned about provo craft's cricut cutting machines. They're amazing machines which take a good deal of work from tons of jobs, they do not call for a computer to utilize, and they're so straightforward and intuitive to understand much we could know them! If you have used then you most likely have seen just how much fun they could be, but have you ever wondered how to earn money doing what you really love?

Making cash out of the fire is really a dream of most, however they often think that it's too difficult and give up. The fact remains that doing so is not all that hard! The only limitation is the creativity and that which it's possible to create. Here's a few tips to get you started with wondering how to earn some cash with your hobby:

Decorate themed parties

Children like to have themed celebrations. When it's a pokemon celebration, a bakugan birthday celebration, a disney character costume party, children just love them. You might easily earn some cash by creating decoration packs for these sorts of occasions. Print and cut out a lot of different sized decorations, so create customized title tags the children can stick , make playing cards or even personality cards that the children can collect and exchange with one another.

Custom cards and invitations

Who does not adore a personalized thank you card or invitation? It demonstrates that many of love and thought has gone into them. Should you love doing so, why don't you sell some of the creations to produce a little cash at precisely the exact same moment? It's actually surprising how a lot of folks would really like to get a custom made card or invitation created because of their birthdays, birthdays, get-togethers, along with exceptional occasions. Fairly often you neighborhood arts and crafts shop will likewise be inclined to set your creations on display and also market them for their clients. Obviously, they frequently have a cut, but it also saves you the time of needing to go outside and find individuals.

Custom scrapbook layouts

Scrapbooking can edge on an obsession with us. We are constantly trying to create that ideal page design, or locate that perfect touch which can make our scrapbooks that better. You can use the cricut system to create expire cuts of scrapbook page designs and then sell them to other fans on your own. If it's your passion then it'll not be any difficulty coming up with a few to-die-for layouts!

Make a site

You can consistently sell your items online. Nowadays it's really simple to generate a web site. Proceed to blogger.com and register to get a free site, then having just a little practice it's possible to produce a wonderful little site featuring all of the wonderful products that you offer. Place it onto a business card (also free with tons of these online offers on the market) and move it out to anyone that you meet. They are easily able to see all you provide in 1 location and place an order.

All these are only a couple of suggestions for you to begin

making cash with your hobbies. Do not hesitate and believe you're not great enough or it's too hard. Just begin wanting, and you might end up amazed at how great your attempts turn out.

CHAPTER THREE
TYPES OF CRICUT

Cricut Cartridges - Forms and Programs With Cricut Machines

C ricut cartridges are mainly the core of a cricut cutting edge machine, which can be put within the cutter system to form the layout as the consumer wants into a bit of paper.

A wide selection of cartridges can be found on the market all around the earth, although not each one these cartridges operate with all sorts of machines. As an example, the cricut cartridge operates with cricut machines just, and it's the vital element whereby crafters and musicians can create many designs in lovely colors and fashions.

With the fluctuations in printing technologies, a selection of cartridges are introduced recently with more packages to pick from compared to prior ones. The two primary sorts of printer cartridges accessible are: that the ink (utilized from the ink-jet printer)laser cartridges are utilized in laser printers. In the instance of all cricut machines, they still utilize ink-jet printers just.

All roughly cricut ink cartridges:

In the start, cricut ink cartridges were just available in dark, however after some time, a few different colors were released. Afterwards, together with advancement in printing technology, ink cartridges have been created, and attempts have been made to present different font styles, layout and colors for forming contours, too.

The key to success of this cricut system, is the usage of different and special kinds of cartridges that empower users to acquire cut and creative in almost any font, layout, color and fashion.

The general types of cricut cartridges are:

* font cartridge: it includes full alphabets, numbers and other symbols together with font styles as well as other font organizing contours. A few of the favorite all-year seasonal and around cartridges comprise little young, jasmine, teardrop, lyrical characters, pumpkin carving for Halloween, thanksgiving holiday, winter wonderland for your Christmas season, etc.,.

* shape cartridge: it includes many different shapes including boxes, tags and bags, animal, sports, newspaper dolls etc..

* licensed cartridge: it enables users to acquire the cut made with favorite figures such as Disney's micky mouse, hello kitty, pixar toy story, etc..

* classmate cartridge: as its name implies, is specifically

created for classroom functions, which includes classroom fonts, shapesand classroom layout, visual analysis program, suggestions and expressions of educators, etc..

* solutions cartridge: it costs less than the remainder. The contours include welding, baseball, soccer, campout, etc..

The broad collection of cricut cartridges, also as mentioned above, provide crafters, particularly young consumers, an opportunity to experiment with their artistic skills without the support of a computer, whereas the cricut ink cartridge which makes it simpler for them to create designs in a variety of shapes and colors.

Selecting The Ideal Cricut For You

Before you buy your very first cricut, it is important to think about all probable alternatives to decide on the very best machine to match your crafting needs.

First, you must stock up to the fundamentals, such as cricut ribbon and picture capsules. These capsules can come in a variety of topics to showcase and commemorate any event, like holidays, holidays or forthcoming events. You'll also require a huge quantity of coloured paper and a pad on which to reduce that contrasts to the dimensions of your system.

If you're an avid scrapbooker, then you ought to check into buying a first cricut cutter or even the cricut expression. This system will cut shapes, letters and themes to decorate your videos. You might even decorate bulletin boards, posters, party decorations, greeting cards or invitations of any sort. The cutters can also reduce cloth too. It's encouraged that you starch that the cloth first so as to generate the project as simple as possible to your system to finish. The gap between both is straightforward. The cricut 12 is a brand new, 12" x 24" version of the first cricut. This system makes it easier to make large-scale jobs at a sizable quantity - should you've got the right quantity of paper. Font and picture cartridges may be utilized in the two machines.

Have you heard of this cricut cake? This useful product is designed to cut nearly anything for baked products, such as frosting sheets, gum paste, fondant, cookie dough, tortillas, baking soda, chewing gum and the majority of other soft foods substances. Whatever material you choose to use must be involving 1/16" and also 1/8" thick. Maintain the blade clean constantly so as to make sure the very best cut possible.

Another favorite cricut alternative is your cricut cuttle bug. This system is modest. It merely cuts paper that's 6 inches wide and weighs just 7 lbs. The cuttlebug is mainly useful for cutting and embossing particular crafts. This really is the best method to decorate several greeting cards invitations. Once you include a selection of colored expires, then the cuttlebug is going to be prepared to emboss straight away. These dies will also be harmonious with sizzix, big shot and thin cuts machines, that serve a similar function.

Why are you curious and creating your personal t-shirts

and cloth designs? Cricut also created the Yudu for all those crafters that love screen-printing and producing their own layouts. The Yudu enables its owners to attach to some laser ink jet printer and generate a layout to screen-print onto virtually anything! Yudus are used for straps, handbags, photograph frames, and shoes - you name it.

Finally, in the event you would like to nourish your newfound cricut obsession, then go right ahead and buy one of those newest cricut gypsys. This useful, hand-held apparatus will keep your ribbon cartridges for simple portable usage. You're able to design from anyplace on the move, in the physician's office, even while on holiday, or merely sitting on your sofa. Anything you plan onto the gypsy is totally transferable to a cricut device for cutting edge. Should you save your layout, it may be linked to some of your cricut apparatus and published at a later moment.

This is a succinct overview of a number of the cutting edge machines cricut presently sells. Because you can see there's a fantastic assortment of machines to get whichever specific kind of craft that you wish to concentrate on. 1 thing is for certain. Whichever machine you select you will have many hours of inspiration and fun producing and creating your own crafting projects.

Although, apparently all of the versions of cricut cutting machines operate in a similar method to some extent using a little bit of variation on precisely the exact same design and characteristics, the cricut design has emerged as a versatile system which has changed the crafting sector by introducing a few new features that improve its functionality.

The cricut machine empowers users to reduce different letters, shapes and phrases in to fine dimensions such as classroom décor, signage, scrapbooks, and much more.

Characteristics Of Cricut Expression machine:

- it's quite simple to work with.

- The Cricut Expression Cartridge does not require a computer as it includes Plantin School Book and Accent Essentials.

- The whole library of present Cricut Cartridge may be utilized.

- It empowers users to decrease figures from 1/4 inches from dimension to around thrilling 11-1/2 inches.

- It includes LCD display that's easy to see and reveals precisely what's being typed.

- Cut landscape and portrait dimensions.

- The program supplies a number mode to pick the amount of cuts that the consumer needs of these chosen on the screen.

- The auto-fill manner can help to fill pages using as many characters as will fit on the specific page.

- By employing this Cricut Expression Cartridge present library that the user may utilize a vast selection of creative attributes in precisely the exact same cut according to choice.

- The built in paper saver mode can help you to occupy the smallest amount of space possible in the newspaper.

- The line-return work will help to acquire precise spacing by producing line breaks in every single cut.

- Fit-to-length along with fit-to-page works readily set how big the duration of a chosen cut on every page.

- The other side permits users to acquire a flipped-mode picture cut of their selected shape.

- It comes in several distinct languages: French, English, German and Spanish - its produced in China, also has a 90 day guarantee.

What Makes the Cricut Expression Machine Much Better Than The Rest?

There are certain attributes the cricut cutter features that makes it distinct from other Cricut machines:

- It's bigger in dimension than many others.

- Compared with other machines it may cut much bigger designs around 23-1/2 inches in complete, which empowers the user to make banner layouts, too.

- As anticipated, with enhanced attributes, the cutter also comprises a high price tag, too.

Despite all of the gaps together with other existing machines that the fantastic news isit has some resemblance with the old one which makes it increasingly useful. This specific Cricut Machine employs exactly the exact same cartridge as other cutters, so therefore, an individual may update his present Cricut into a new one and utilize his/her assortment of older Cartridges. Even though the Cutter comes with its Cricut Expression Cartridge, undoubtedly, it provides you with additional design choices.

Cricut Scrapbooking Machine Review

If you're an avid scrapbooker, you need to get one of those machines. They're the greatest garbage booking enthusiast's buddy. They operate simply by loading a cartridge to the machine and picking out literally tens of thousands of possibilities for the decorating ideas.

The phrases and also the border may be an incredible 11 1/2 inches . The cartridges you buy on the Cricut scrap washing machine will provide you the choice of picking from over 250 layouts. And that isn't all. The dimensions of these layouts are from 1 inch to 5 1/2 inches.

How a lot of men and women may create their garbage book as beautiful as possible using this superb machine to provide you with professional results each moment? The broad variety of shapes, letters, layouts, and phrases to grow your scrap book will probably help it become a precious book for several years to come.

This is a fantastic gift idea for anybody who loves crap booking. The newspaper slides and everything you do is push a single button. The machine manages the remainder. The portability of this Cricut is yet another notable feature. It weighs just 7 pounds that's excellent for carrying along on a visit from town for a couple of days or into some buddy's home that shares your own hobby.

Another in the household of Cricut products is your Private Electronics Cutter that has exactly the very same dimensions as the standard Cricut machine however, it's the choice of permitting you to cut out of a quarter of a inch up to 11.5 inches. The Personal Electronic Cutter includes a blade which enables cutting edge from eight distinct ways.

The Cuts you are able to make with this particular eight way blade are amongst others these reductions:

Portrait

Fit to page

Auto fill

Center Stage

Flip function

All these features aren't on the normal Cricut cutter. The advancements which were created are great additions like the display screen was improved along with the layout appears to be much skinnier.

Cricut Expressions is a bit larger than the standard Cricut. It wasn't supposed to be portable as the other two; rather it's to remain put to a desk or inside a meeting area. There could be gaps in dimensions and the capability to choose the Cricut Expressions filler with you however all of them use exactly the identical size capsules as well as the very same blades.

When you need letters, numbers, shapes, or whatever else cut to the scrap book or anything you want them the cricut expression is the cutter. The capability to mix and match with the attributes on the very first cut is among the remarkable elements of this machine.

There is no demand to get a computer since everything you'll need is at the cartridge which you load in the machine. An LCD display will show you exactly what directions you're typing in and also the preferences for speech and dimensions are changeable.

If you enjoy scrap booking and wish to obtain all your books so and put up precisely how you would like them to seem, you are going to need to try these Cricut crap booking machines.

That Scrapbooking Machine If You Select?

If you're thinking of getting a cutting edge machine to better your crafting projects, you've probably already discovered there are a vast array of machines from which to pick. How can you select which machine is going to be the right for you? Cost, obviously, is the largest deciding factor, however, where would you go then? Do you desire a manual system or a digital system? Would you wish to get individual expires, cartridges with numerous pictures, or would you desire the extreme flexibility of a pc based system? Listed below are a number of details about the sorts of cutting machines out there.

Manual Die Cutting Machines

Manual Cutting machines need no power and are managed by hand. They're the cheapest of your alternatives. A number of those manual cutters comprise the Cuttlebug, the Sizzix, as well as also the Quickut Squeeze or even the Quickut Revolution. You'll have to acquire individual dies for all these machines, one for each form that you would like to reduce. The Cuttlebug, among the most recent versions of guide cutters, will utilize expires from many manufactures and contains a wonderful embossing attribute. The Cuttlebug along with the Sizzix will reduce pretty thick materials such as chipboard, fun felt and foam. The Sizzix, nevertheless, is among the earliest die cutting machines offered and can be limited to a single or two fonts. Every one these components are mobile for carrying along to plants or holidays.

Digital Cutting Machines

You can choose digital cutting machines which stand alone or those that need the usage of a pc. The Cricut along with the Cricut Expression don't need to be plugged into the pc. These machines utilize cartridges designed especially for all these machines. Each cartridge be bought separately but includes several pictures. There's optional applications available to your Cricut should you would like to enhance the flexibility of those systems.

There are several computer-based versions out there for home usage, such as the Quickz Silhouette, Xyron Wishblade, and Craft Robo. All three of those machines are essentially the same, letting you cut some true type font you've got on your PC. The Wishbone is the most costly of the three, however it will include additional designs and applications. Your layout choices are wide open using one or more of these machines. In case you have problems learning precisely how to run the machine, you will find support groups on the internet where you'll discover seasoned crafters keen to assist. You could even save your layouts on the internet or email them . Needless to say, those machines are more costly than standalone or manual machines.

Which Cutting machine is most suitable for you?

Now you have to decide which cutting edge machine would be the ideal fit for your needs. Do your own research and be truthful with yourself. Just how much are you ready to make investments? How long do you must use your device? Can it be too hard for you to understand the methods for the more complex versions? Will buying person dies or capsules limit your imagination and be more expensive in the future than a larger up front investment? As soon as you answer these questions, then you'll be more prepared to opt for a cutting machine which will best fit your own needs.

With Cricut Cutting Machines On The Craft Projects

More and increasing numbers of folks are deciding to create their own scrapbooking stuff, invitations and cards. These do-it-yourself choices allow considerably more room for customization compared to their mass produced choices. Not just are homemade invitations much more customizable, but they also cost much less than shop - bought options. Circut private cutting machines also make it feasible for those who have minimal time and much less expertise to create professional looking craft jobs anytime.

Cricut Cutting machines can be found anyplace in craft shops in addition to some department stores which contain craft and art segments. On the other hand, the very best prices are usually located on the internet. For your occasional do-ityourselfer, the entry level version, with easily available sale costs of about $100 is more than adequate. It's more than capable of generating a huge number of distinct shape mixes and requires very little maintenance. More seasoned crafters, or people who handle home companies that produce personalized paper products, might discover that bigger versions are more in accordance with their demands.

All these machines are semi automatic, and much simpler to use than manual paper cutters. Typically, they could cut through very heavy paper stock, allowing scrapbookers to make designs with many different shades and textures. For advice about the best way best to use a machine, there are a range of websites offering information from frequent amateur customers. They may be an important source of the inspiration and information, showing the way the machine might be best employed. When these websites are a terrific destination for people that are only beginning, the very best feature of a house Cricut machine would be your capability to make completely one-of-a-kind webpages. Experiment with new form and colour combinations to make something distinctive and memorable.

Cricut Cutting Machines Are Flexible Enough For Use For Any Type Of Craft Job.

Make professional searching scrapbooks using Circut Personal Cutting Machines

A cricut cutting machine is essential have for any scrapbooker. These machines make it possible for consumers to cut paper to some range of intriguing contours, making personalizing each page at a scrapbook simple and enjoyable. Made to be modest enough to bring with you once you travel, they'll occupy little space in your house and may be carried with you to get almost any scrapbooking celebrations you might attend. They're the ideal tool for everybody who's searching for a user friendly way of producing unique boundaries, inserts or alternative page vases.

Cricut machines can produce shapes which are anywhere from 1" to over just 5" tall. Simple to alter metal cutting patterns have been utilized to make uniform contours in many kinds of craft paper. These forms may be used to include custom decoration, festive contours or intriguing boundaries that can reflect the information of every webpage. As many distinct thicknesses of card stock might be used, scrapbookers ought to be conscious that paper at a milder grade might cause the blades to boring faster. This usually means that you should constantly keep a tab on the sharpness of the blade and then replace them if needed to keep great outcomes.

A cricut machine isn't a little investment. Prices begin at about $100 online, which might put this cutting edge machine from reach for a few. But when taking into consideration the price of buying packs of pre-cut shapes and letters, most dedicated scrapbook fans do discover the system will eventually pay for itself. In addition, it can be utilized for additional newspaper based crafts, like making custom invitations, gift tags and cards. The cricut firm has a good reputation in the trading globe, and their products are know to be durable, therefore no replacement ought to be required, in spite of heavy usage.

Searching For Your Cricut Accent Essentials Cartridge?

The cricut accent essentials is among these die cut capsules which everybody wants. But it can be tough to find since it's sold exclusively using all the expression machine. If you don't have the expression, or if you bought a cricut system which didn't incorporate this particular cartridge, there's very good news if it's in your record of must-haves. For those who know where to look, you can purchase this, and in a pretty decent cost! Or, if you're particularly thrifty, you might even have the ability to get it at no cost. Continue reading to learn just how...

1. Create a trade.

If you truly need the accent essentials cartridge, but don't wish to cover this, you might have the ability to exercise a transaction, either temporary or permanent, together with somebody who possesses this particular cartridge. If you frequently attend plants or have a set of record buddies you want to meet up , inquire to see whether anybody will be inclined to figure out a transaction.

Many scrapbookers also see forums and other internet

places, like sites, to go over their own projects. Join a discussion and render an easy article, detailing exactly what cartridges you'd be ready to part with to be able to work out a market. Forums and sites are fantastic places to place this kind of petition, due to the amount of individuals seeing these online meeting areas. You could be amazed by the amount of answers you get.

2. Have a look at classified advertising.

You can take a look at your regional classified ads to determine if anybody has the product you would like listed available. Even better however, extend your search to internet classified listings to find out if anybody has got the cartridge available on the market. Craigslist along with other similar sites make it possible for users to post things they wish to sell. Unlike neighborhood classified listings, several internet vendors don't have any trouble sending things to buyers which don't reside within their regional area.

3. Visit online stores.

Even though cricut doesn't market the accent essentials cartridge separately, and you won't have the ability to discover it in retail shops, online shoppers have additional options. Several internet retailers swap out the capsules contained with machines so as to personalize orders to their clients. Because of swapping, a number of these online shops have this distinctive cartridge readily available for sale.

4. Assess online auctions.

Online auction websites, like ebay, are also excellent places to search down hard-to-find products. Many buyers can pick up things for a fraction of the price.

As you are able to see, that the cricut accent essentials cartridge really isn't really that hard to discover. Whether you're seeking to produce a transaction or to buy it, then you need to not have any trouble finding it in a cost you prepared to cover.

CHAPTER FOUR
HOW TO START CRICUT

The Cricut Machine

The Cricut system is a really renowned invention. It's helped scrapbookers and lots of individuals with their demands not just restricted in the scrapbook creating planet but also to other aspects too. It's to be mentioned however that the 1 sector it's helped is on the scrapbooking kingdom. From the fantastic old dark ages, even if you weren't proficient at carvings or in case you didn't understand how to compose, your favorite moment goes down the drain.

Those two would be the sole means of maintaining the memories back afterward. It might appear crude and ancient to us back then, it was that they needed. Now, we've got everything set up to the preservation of someone's memories and also we all to Father Technology.

When a scrapbooker makes the decision to make a scrapbook, that the layout is almost always a key consideration. Before, picking a design can cause migraines of epic proportions but today is another story. The cricut system to be mentioned is only accountable for cutting edge newspapers, vinyl, and cloth according to a particular pattern or layout. The design or pattern can be made or edited by means of a software application known as the Cricut Design Studio.

If you're searching for simple and well - recognized designs which are already built - in, you proceed for capsules that are secondhand. There's not any limitation to everything you could think of using the layouts which are already set up. The golden rule would be to allow your creativity go crazy. This really is a tool which any aspiring scrapbooker must possess. So far is it? The prices generally start at $299 and will go up based on the version which you pick.

It might appear to be substantial sum of money however, the expense is well worth it. But if you wish to employ the additional effort to learn to locate a fantastic deal, you're more than welcome about this. The world wide web is almost always a wonderful place to get some excellent bargains, you simply have to look. There is Amazon, eBay, so a lot more.

The cricut machine has lots of uses besides being a cutter of layouts to get a scrapbook. The layouts itself may be used to make different things like greeting cards, wall decorations, and more. You simply have to believe creatively. There are not any limitations and when there are, they're only a figment of your own imagination.

The Cricut Machine - A Short and Intimate Appearance

When you think about building a scrapbook, the very first

thing comes in your head is exactly what pictures to put. That is fairly simple as all you want to do would be to pick images that highlight a particular event or happening on your lifetime. After this was completed, at this point you should think of the layout to the scrapbook. Again, this can be quite simple as everything that you have to do is base your choice on whatever occasion has been depicted on your own pictures. Let us take for instance, a wedding day.

Pick a design which will transfer that audience back in time and relive everything transpired throughout your wedding day. Common sense is everything you may need here. The next thing is to produce the layout. How can you take action? Can you do it ? No is the reply to those above query. You do so through the usage of a cricut machine.

The cricut machine is a fantastic creation. This poor boy is able to help you cut paper, cloth, and vinyl sheets to whatever pattern you would like. The actual production of these designs may be achieved via software tools like the cricut layout studio or via capsules using pre - engineered designs assembled in to them. Therefore, if you're enthusiastic scrap booker, this system is essential have.

How exactly how does one cost? Well every unit comes with an average cost of $299 with greater versions having larger price tags. However there are means by which you'll be able to find a less expensive price. In case you've got a pc with internet, proceed browse and hunt for great bargains and inexpensive cutting machines that are secondhand. EBay is a good place to begin with.

Recall nevertheless, that carrying purchases through eBay can take dangers so that you need to be certain you check out each of the vendor's profiles which you may want to participate in. If you're the fantastic conventional shopper who'll never devote to internet purchasing, you could do this old - school and then buy from a mall through earnings or anything else similar.

The cricut machine has additionally many applications which extend far beyond the domain of scrapbooking. Given the amount of layouts which might be in your own cartridge or software application, you may always utilize them to make cricut calendars, hangings such as partitions, and greeting cards for special events. Your creativity is the one thing which may limit your creativity.

Marsha Brascher was crafting for several decades. She loves the challenge of producing cutting documents, and that she understands what is needed to make handmade crafts having the most complex of designs.

Cricut Suggestions - Tips That May Help You to Get Started

Capturing memories onto a virtual camera, even an HD camera, and a voice recorder make life much more purposeful. When there's a unique moment which you would like to catch and be in a position to return to at any certain time, you are able to certainly do this so easily with the assistance of these instruments. However, pictures continue to be the favorite medium by the majority of people. If you wish to put together those images and compile them onto a distinctive memorabilia, then you flip into scrapbooking.

Scrapbooking is a technique of preservation of thoughts that's been in existence for quite some time and it's evolved up to now better. Previously, the invention of a single scrapbook was a monumentally crazy job. But now, with the Creation of devices like the Cricut cutting edge machine, matters are made simpler. If you're Looking to Developing a scrapbook, this poor boy is the instrument for you. There Are Lots of good cricut thoughts out there you can make the most of.

Scrapbooks are only some of many cricut thoughts on the market. This instrument, if you understand how to optimize it makes it possible for you to create things which go past scrapbooking for example calendars. If you buy a cricut cartridge, then there are a slew of layouts uploaded in every and every one. All these pre- made themes may be used for a whole lot of items like hangings for partitions, image frames, picture frames, and greeting cards for many seasons.

Just your creativity will limit your advancement using a cricut machine. Together with calendars, you are able to design every month to represent the weather, the disposition, and exceptional events which are connected with that. The cricut machine will take care of this. But in case one cartridge doesn't have the layout that search, you may always go and purchase. It's that simple!

Cricut machines may be a little expensive with all the cost starting at $299. That's pretty hefty for anybody to begin with. Be a smart buyer. You may always turn into the world wide web to seek out great bargains on cricut machines. Purchasing from eBay may also be a terrific move but can take several dangers if you aren't experienced with eBay. In case you're quite worried about this, you always have the option to await a purchase to occur at one of the regional malls and buy out there since it will probably have a guarantee.

Those are among the numerous great cricut thoughts on the market. Calendars so many more could be made with the usage of this machine that is fantastic. Bear in mind, only your imagination will restrict what you could do.

Earning Your Cricut Mat Sticky Again

Are you aware you don't have to obtain a new mat every-time your mat reductions it is stickiness?

When your mat reaches the point at which nothing will adhere and your newspaper only moves around if you attempt to reduce, then it is time to"re-stickify" (is that a phrase??) Your mat. This is a really straightforward procedure and you'll be stunned at how well it's working!

- Step 1- Carry your mat into your sink. Utilize some hot

water, a couple drops of dish soap and a green scotch brite washing machine. Scrub your mat beneath the tepid water. You will begin to find the small pieces of newspaper and filthy sticky grime begin to come off. You might even utilize the scrapper which came on the Cricut tool kit that will assist you scrap away some of the gunk also. Keep scrubbing before all of that additional layer of gunk is eliminated. Based upon your mat, then this can strip it all of the way to the vinyl with no stickiness left or right there can still be a little quantity of stickiness. Either way would be fine.

• Step 2- You then wish to let it airdry or use your own hair dryer. Do not use a towel to wash it since it is going to leave lint .

• Step 3- Permit that airdry for approximately one hour. It is ready to rock & roll up back again. I've done this on my mats and over again.

• Measure 4- Then, have a wide tipped ZIG 2 way glue pen and use paste in lines round the entire mat.

• Measure 5- Permit dry for 1 hour before implementing the translucent sheet back .

Cricut Sale - Enhancing Your Abilities

If a man was great at something, could he do it at no cost? Sometimes, the response will be"yes". However, if it's a skill which you feel can deliver food onto the table you want to capitalize on it. Therefore, in case you've got a cricut cutting tool, a program, and a knack for managing layouts and patterns, then this may be a better opportunity for you to measure and begin earning. This is where it is possible to find a cricut sale.

The cricut machine may be utilized to cut the layouts that you pick from the applications tool. With the support of this cricut style studio, it is possible to eventually discover the layout that you search for a great deal of stuff. However, before we proceed any farther with the idea of ways to acquire a cricut purchase, let's understand the various applications of the designs and patterns which we get out of our applications.

Greeting cards are among the most frequent items that the layouts are utilized for. The cover is easily the most likely recipient of those designs or layouts. Therefore, if you currently have an issue in your mind; plug on your personal computer, activate the program and search for your layout. In case the cover copes with a Christmas motif then search for layout that will tell the story of Christmas. It's that simple. Consequently, if you understand those who desire their gift cards customized, then this is definitely the most opportune time to you allow the company person in you talk.

The production of calendars is an additional fantastic undertaking which you're able to participate in using all the designs and layouts which come from your own software. Utilize the layouts to breathe life to every month using the design/s which you opt for. If we're speaking about December, subsequently select designs which have a Christmas theme for this. Last but not least, yet another one of the most frequent applications of the program patterns and layouts are available on decorations for partitions. There are not any limitations to what you could do this so the essential thing is to simply let your creativity go crazy on the decoration you may produce.

So that you have it. As soon as you master the craft of producing the three which were only mentioned, you'll have a cricut sale very quickly. But naturally, you also will require determination and endurance to produce this work.

Crafting Hobbyists - With the Cricut Machine

Crafting is among the most well-known hobbies in the world these days. You can find many men, women and even kids who like crafting and a few who make a professional living from it. There are tons of unique instruments, gear and software applications available to assist these crafting fans take advantage of their moment.

The cricut machine is merely that. It's a digital cutter which aids with newspaper crafts. With only a touch of a button it is possible to make amazing designs and receive assistance with crafts such as home decor, art, paper crafting and much more. The device is quite simple to navigate and utilize so the one thing that you truly need to be worried about is being imaginative and allowing your imagination run rampant.

There is no demand for a pc to utilize the Cricut device. All you will need is a conventional electric outlet to plug it into and you're prepared to go. Before you begin it's helpful to bring a little bit of time and make more comfortable with the equipment. Have a peek at the newspaper feed to comprehend how everything operates.

The on button, then cut button and stop switch will be grouped with the right of this device, the newspaper feed in the rear.

To begin, first determine what crafts that you wish to perform on. Put a cricut cartridge to the system and you also get to select from various layouts, sizes and receive every detail from the way. There are hundreds and hundreds of possibilities so that the layouts you can produce with your crafting will be infinite.

There is a user manual which is included with the device when you buy it give this a browse through in the event that you're experiencing any issues. The Cricut system is a priceless investment for any crafter who chooses their hobby seriously.

Three Approaches to Boost Your Growing Time

The cricut electronic mail machine paired using all the cricut design studio applications has opened a completely new universe of designing chances for scrapbookers and cardmakers alike. Though a lot people have plenty of materials and tools, the 1 thing we appear to be lacking over every other is the time. It's crucial to utilize the time we can see into the fullest if we would like to finish additional jobs. Here are 3 approaches to make the most of your time creating.

1. Maintain appropriate maintenance on your own machine, mat, blade and gear.

If you spend few added minutes it can take to maintain your system in good shape it will help save you money and time in the long run. The two largest culprits appear to be the blade along with the cutting mat. Change out your blade if needed to prevent from wasting paper with ripped or less-than-perfect cuts and also the time that it requires to re-cut your own images. If you attempt to extend out using your mat also long that the newspapers will start to move and slip as the device cuts. It is more than worthwhile to execute the age old information about doing things correctly the first time.

2. Become knowledgeable about the individuals who may assist you. Getting to be aware of the tools available to assist you may help you save time once you get stuck together with the equipment and applications. The most significant source in my view is your Cricut message boards. There are a few terrific folks on the market more than prepared to answer virtually any question you've got and assist with ideas.

3. Do not reinvent the wheel. If you don't merely delight in playing and designing with the application, there is no reason

to recreate a document somebody else has already produced. There are many sites and websites where other Cricut users discuss the jobs as well as the corresponding documents they've designed.

There is No reason to devote valuable time designing cuttings from scratch if somebody has put it to the net that you utilize. Even when you simply use the foundation of this layout as a starting point for incorporating your own developments, you will still save a whole lot of time rather than attempting to determine how to make the document in the very start. 1 thing to bear in mind is to always give credit where credit is due, even in the event that you decide to alter the document in 1 manner or the other.

Spend a small amount of additional time up front by maintaining your resources at tip-top shape, becoming to understand where to locate assistance, and with other people's layouts as soon as you're able to. If you do, if you sit down to focus on a project you might just realize you have additional time to really finish it than you ever believed.

CHAPTER FIVE
TIPS ON HOW TO GET
STARTED WITH CRICUT

25 Tips & Tricks To Get Cricut Newbies

Ok, so a number of these tips and tips are VERY simple, and therefore are for the complete novice to Cricut machines. But be certain to scan through the entire list since we guarantee there is a hint or hint with your title on it!

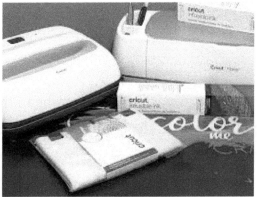

1. Register To Cricut Accessibility

If you really want to get the maximum from owning a Cricut Research Air two, we then advocate subscribing to Cricut Accessibility . It's possible to pay a monthly charge of about $10, or even a yearly fee that proves to be marginally cheaper a month.

Cricut access provides you access to 30,000+ images, 1000's of jobs and more than 370 fonts. If you're likely to use your own Cricut a whole lot, then that can save a great deal of cash than if you should get every undertaking and picture separately.

Plus it is less of a hassle to cover a set rate compared to stressing about just how much cash you are actually spending projects! It provides up! Make your money's worth from your Cricut by creating the amazing Design Space jobs.

2. De-tack Your Cutting Mat

De-tack Your own Cricut cutting mat a bit!

The Explore Air 2 typically includes The green normal cutting mat, although the Maker generally will come with all the grim light clasp mat. You put your stuff on the mat prior to placing it in the machine.

The green cutting mat is fairly tacky when new! Once you peel off the plastic cap off, then you can put a clean, sterile t-shirt within the mat to be able to prime it to your very first job. It is quite tough to acquire that the cardstock off, even in the event that you have all of the resources, when it is in its entire stickiness! It's simple to hurt the project whilst attempting to get off it.

You should not have this issue with the grim light clasp mat, which means you might also buy that for your card and paper jobs rather than de-tacking the mat.

3. Maintain Your Cutting Mat Covers

The cutting mats Include a Plastic shield . This may be pulled away and place back easily.

We maintained our pay and put it back our mat once we are done with this it retains the mat tacky and clean longer!

4. Fixing The Cricut Cutting Mat

Every once and a while (or even every Time you use it), provide your cutting mat a wash over with a few baby wipes.

The non-alcohol water packs without aroma are greatest. This can help keep it free of creating up using cardstock and plastic residue out of cuttingedge, and the normal family dust and lint drifting around.

5. Get The Ideal Tools

It includes a useful instrument, also a scraper, tweezers, a spatula along with scissors. It's particularly beneficial to have the weeding tool if you're considering cutting adhesive plastic or heat transport vinyl.

6. The Cricut Scoring Stylus

So a number of the card jobs ask that you get the scoring stylus. I didn't purchase one with my equipment initially, and thus needed a debilitating wait for it to arrive until I really could go to a better jobs. If you purchased your system as part of a package, it might possess the scoring stylus contained, so double check .

7. Start with The Sample Project

Once your device arrives, begin with The sample job.

The research air two and maker include sample stuff for an initial job. Unless you purchase a Cricut Bundle, you get the minimum number of stuff to do this small thing, however it is ideal to begin simple!

Instead of attempting to do anything big and elaborate, simply start here in order to find a sense of how things work software and hardware wise.

8. Evaluation Cuts

After doing your own jobs it may be sensible to perform a test cut prior to doing the entire thing. If the blade has been set too low it will destroy your cutting mat. When it's too large it might just cut marginally during your vinyl, cardstock, etc. and mess up your materials.

Doing a test trimming may involve asking your system to cut a little circle. Check the atmosphere is correct and make adjustments if needed.

9. Alter Pen Lids After Utilization

It is very important to have the lid it Asap after you have finished using it that it will not dry out. They're too costly to waste. The neat thing about the Design Space jobs is the fact that it frequently prompts one to set the lid back !

10. Aged Cricut Cartridges

Do not forget to hook up any older Cartridges you might have obtained from a former device to your account. This is a rather easy process, as displayed below.

Each chance can simply be connected after, so if you are taking a look at purchasing some second hand, then affirm that this has not been achieved yet!

Besides utilizing the right tools to eliminate your cardstock or plastic in the leading mat, there's just another trick to getting off it.

Rather than peeling your project from the mat, that could lead to curling (or overall mangling), peel away the mat from the undertaking. Bend the mat from the card instead of the other way round.

12. Purchase The Deep Cut Blade

There is nothing worse than placing your heart upon a project and then finding you do not have the ideal tools!

The heavy cut blade lets One to cut deeper leather, card, chipboard and much more. This blade works with all the Explore Air 2. It's necessary to not just get the bladebut the blade casing too.

13. Totally free SVG documents

You do not only have to use layouts in the design space shop. You may either make your SVG documents, or utilize other free SVG documents that may be found all around the world wide web.

14. Alternative Pens For Cricut

You are not stuck just with Cricut Pens in Cricut Machines!

You may use Cricut pencil adapters (such as that 1) so as to utilize any pencil with the Maker or Air Conditioning 2. Look at these Cricut Etsy Finds for much more weird and Terrific inventions for Cricut!

15. Load Mat Correctly

Ensure that your mat is properly filled before you begin cutting. It ought to slide beneath the rollers. Your device will probably just begin cutting ahead of the cap of the grid onto the mat or perhaps not if it has not been loaded directly.

16. Utilize Free Fonts

You will find so many free font websites for one to begin using!

Browse the internet to get a listing of free fonts for Cricut. You only download the fontand install it on your own computer and it'll appear on your Cricut Design Space (see next tip).

Regrettably, among the greatest fonts, Samantha Font, isn't readily available free of charge, however check that connection to learn where you are able to get it to get the very best price!

17. Installing Themes

After installing a ribbon to your computer, you might want to sign up and back to Cricut Design Space prior to your font will appear there. You might even have to restart your pc in order for it to appear (mine would not appear without restarting my pc).

For more information read the way to set up fonts from Cricut Design Space.

18. Fixing Blades

Like that which, Cricut blades utilize out. If the reductions are no more so smooth and powerful it is time for a shift. Other Indicators that you Want a brand new blade comprise:

§ Tearing plastic or card

§ Lifting or pulling off vinyl off the backing sheet

§ Not cutting all of the way through (ensure your trimming setting is right too)

You can buy brand new blades Amazon or see that Cricut Blade Guide for much more purchasing choices.

19. Whenever Your Favorite Looses Its Stick

Cleaning your mat is 1 approach for slightly more life from your cutting mat. However, if it is beyond this, and you haven't purchased a brand new cutting mat still, you may tape off your plastic or card to maintain it in position.

Evidently, you do not need to tape over a place that's having to be trimmed down a few sides must perform the job. Even a moderate tack painters tape is ideal to this undertaking, and ought not to harm your cardstock.

20. Cricut's Custom Cut Settings

The Explore Air two includes 7 preset Choices on the dial:

§ Paper

§ Vinyl

§ Iron-on

§ Light cardstock

§ Cardstock

§ Bonded fabric

§ Poster board

If the material you're cutting is not on this listing, there's a customized option that you'll be able to pick on the dialup. Visit Design Space, choose your project and click'Make It'. Then you will have the ability to choose your content by a drop down menu.

Or you may produce a new custom made cloth. You may find more info relating to it on in Cricut's site .

21. Various Blades For Different Materials

Some Folks swear by using different Blades for cutting every substance.

By way of example, using one blade which you merely use for cardstock, and yet another that you merely use for the vinyl. That is because the a variety of stuff will wear otherwise on your own blades. Cutting plastic is simpler on the blade compared to cutting card.

Having a committed blade to get vinyl means that it will remain sharp and ready, instead of having a blade to get all that immediately goes dull then lifts your vinyl!

22. Mirror Your Pictures For HTV

If you're cutting heat transfer vinyl together with your Cricut, then you'll have to mirror your own design!

Once you choose 'Make It' there's a choice to mirror your layout (as seen below), and you'll need to pick this choice for every individual mat!

23. Set HTV The Perfect Way Up

In order to lower heat transport vinyl you'll have to set your vinyl polished side down on the outer mat.

This way the carrier sheet is. Beneath along with the dull plastic side is at the top. It is difficult to determine which side the carrier sheet is around, so remember polished side down and you are going to be OK!

24. Weeding Boxes

If you're cutting a little or intricate layout, or you're cutting a great deal of unique designs on a single sheet of vinyl, so it can help use weeding boxes.

Simply use the square instrument in cricut design room to put a box around your layout and set both components together. Unlock the silhouette at the bottom left corner manipulate it in a rectangle.

This makes weeding easier than weeding several layouts at the same time on the 1 sheet of vinyl, and even simpler than attempting to observe where your layouts are cutting them out individually using scissors.

25. Don't Forget to Establish The Dial

This suggestion sounds like a no brainer; however,how often have I forgotten how to alter the material placing?!

It is this easy thing to overlook -- Particularly once you have finally completed your layout and really wish to get clipping edge! The humorous thing is that Cricut Design Space really tells you exactly what substance that the dial is put into if you're just about to cut a layout -- but it's not difficult to forget that also!

Save the mistake of cutting on Right through to a cutting mat, or perhaps through your cardstock -- check your dialup!

... And today we've a bonus tip!

26! Keep A Source Of Materials

As we mentioned previously, it is a nuisance If you would like to begin a project and you do not have the perfect tools.

As an instance, we have been capable of being with no grading stylus, without the ideal pencil for a job, and with no profound cut blade. However, another hassle is if you would like to do a project and you have run out of glue plastic, HTV or cardstock!

CHAPTER SIX
PRECAUTIONS TO CRICUT MACHINE

Be A Specialist in Locating Affordable Cricut Cartridges

The invention of Cricut machine also has made newspaper crafting a hobby to expire! This system made craftwork easier and more intriguing. It permits you to expire cut shapes and fonts of various sizes from other paper materials in the touch of a button. This system doesn't include affordable Cricut cartridges that are utilized to make your own shapes and fonts.

A Personal Cutter out of Provo Craft will charge you less $299 and also the fancier Cricut Expressions is significantly more costly at $499. Together with the machine include the accessories such as Cricut cartridges that are likewise not easy in the pocket. It's possible to acquire affordable Cricut Cartridges and machines at the world wide web in addition to from additional specialty shop. You only need to know where to search.

By placing a little effort in comparing costs, it's no problem to locate bargains in your Cricut printer machines in addition to cartridges and other accessories. There are lots of craft shops which you are able to visit throughout their voucher specials. JoAnn Fabrics, Michaels and Hobby Lobby are a few of the very popular craft shops which sell Cricut accessories and machines. Look out for your weekly earnings from other community craft shops.

Paper Crafting Pro provides some excellent bargains up to 20 and less. You can't get their pricing in case you don't enroll online. The enrollment, however, isn't totally free. You have to pay $9.99 for your monthly fee. If you're in a company of disposing cartridges, to enroll is a fantastic thing, however, as you've got monthly charges to cover, start looking for different sites which don't charge membership fees.

You may also purchase more affordable Cricut cartridges out of eBay. You're able to score on a brand newchance under $15 buck. Even though you've got to run on the capsules, you simply need to be patient and be inclined to bidding . As a result, you can prevent overpaying for the capsule. Lookout for transport fees. Find vendors who provide free shipment inside the US land. You might even bidding Cricut Cake capsules which generally cost around $100 that you are able to acquire on the internet for $25 or not. Many do not realize that but Cricut Cake capsules may be utilised in almost any Cricut machine.

Oh my scrapbooking is really a site which consistently sells Cricut cartridges in a reduce cost. Their cartridges can charge

$30 and under. You are able to register to their email newsletter and receive coupons for up to 20% off.

There you've got it. It is not really tough to search for affordable Cricut cartridges once you know the best place to look. Always remember: not cover the complete cost of a Cricut chance or for dispatch that prices you over $30.

Device Is ripping or pulling through my stuff

There are several factors that might give rise to a system to rip through substance. Luckily, this issue can normally be solved with a few simple troubleshooting measures. In case a Cricut Maker or Cricut Explore device is ripping or dragging throughout the content, assess the following:

- make certain you have chosen the suitable content placing in Design Space or the Smart Position Dial is about the right setting.

- If you're using the customized setting, make certain that the suitable material is chosen from the drop-down listing.

- Confirm the size and intricacy of this picture. If you're cutting a picture that's quite complicated or little, consider cutting out a simpler or bigger.

- When trimming on a easy picture resolves the matter, consider cutting the intricate image utilizing the customized setting for Cardstock - Intricate Cuts.

- If employing a Cricut Explore Air two or Cricut Maker in Quick Mode, turn Quick Mode away and try your trimming again.

- Eliminate the blade home in the device, then get rid of the blade and also look for any debris within the home or onto the blade.

- Reduce pressure configurations for that substance type from the Manage Custom Materials display by means of 2-4. Get the Manage Custom Materials display through the accounts menu or by choosing Edit Custom Materials at the top from your Mat Preview display once you click on Change Material.

- That might have to be performed 2-3 days to alter the trimming result.

- Try cutting another substance -- like copy paper at the proper setting for this material. It might be an issue with this particular substance which you're working to cut.

- Try with a fresh mat and blade. Both can lead to cut problems.

- When the problem persists after you've completed each these measures, please contact Member Care through a few of the choices below for more help.

CHAPTER SEVEN
THINGS TO KNOW ABOUT
CRICUT

Cricut Comparisons - Which to Buy?

There are currently 5 Cricut machine versions. They're made by the Provo Craft business. How can you know which to purchase? In the event you begin small or move large off the bat? I will offer you the details of every one in easy terms so you can create your own choice on what is right for you. We will discuss the 4 primary machines. There's currently a Cricut Cake system, but it's so much like this Cricut Expression, I am not likely to pay that you especially.

Let us Split down it

Original Cricut: (aka Baby Bug)

- Mat dimensions = 6 x 12

- Could utilize all cartridges

- Can utilize all of blades and housings

- Can utilize markers

- Cuts any size newspaper that suits about the mat

Makes cuts that range from 1 inch to 5-1/2 inches in

dimension, in half inch increments.

Could connect to a PC and use Design Studio or Certainly Cuts lots Computer Software

Cricut Produce: (Type of a hybrid of this Baby Bug and also the saying. It's still modest, but includes a number of the qualities of this Cricut Expression)

- May utilize all cartridges

- May utilize all of blade and housings

- May utilize markers

- Cuts any size newspaper that suits around the mat

- Makes cuts that range from 1/4 inch into 11-1/2 inches in dimension, in quarter inch increments.

- Can link to a PC and use Design Studio or Positive Cuts lots Computer Software

- Has any innovative attribute buttons (reverse, fit to page, match to span, centre stage, etc..)

- Can link to a PC and use Design Studio or Positive Cuts lots Computer Software

Cricut Length:

- Mat dimensions = 12 x 12, or 12 x 24

- Could utilize all cartridges

- Can utilize all of blades and housings

- Could utilize markers

- Cuts any size newspaper that is suitable for on size pad

Makes cuts out of 1/4 inch into 23-1/2 inches in dimension, in quarter inch increments.

Has lots of innovative attribute buttons (reverse, fit to page, match to span, centre stage, etc..)

Has style keys (amount, auto load, portrait, etc..)

Could link to a PC and work with Design Studio or Certain Cuts lots Computer Software

Cricut Picture: (Newest & greatest version. The design of this Cricut machine using a colour printer)

- Mat dimensions = 12 x 12 (unique Dark mat)

- May utilize all cartridges

- Can utilize all of blades and housings

- Cuts or eyeglasses or equally on any size document that suits on mat

- Makes cuts out of 1/4 inch into 11-1/2 inches in dimension, in quarter inch increments

- Has lots of imaginative attributes (turn, fit on page, match to span, centre point, etc..)

- Has manners (amount, auto match, portrait, etc..)

- The device will print the picture and then cut it.

Comes with an LCD display and runs on the stylus for browsing the display

Same Accessories are compatible with machines. The cartridgesblades, tools and markers aren't machine-specific. The cutting pads are the sole thing that change based upon the machine. The new Picture also needs the new mat. The aged green mats won't work with this.

If You're wanting this system for portability, size and weight may be a variable for you.

Weight Dimensions

Private Cricut 7 Lbs. 15.5" x 7" x 7"

Cricut Produce 10.75 Lbs 15.5" x 7" x 7"

Cricut Expression 13.4 Lbs. 21.5" x 7" x 7.75"

Cricut Picture 28 Lbs. 23.5" x 9" x13.5"

Personal and produce are equally small, mobile lightweight machines. If you're taking your endeavors to plants or distinct tasks then you may wish to think about one of these. They're lightweight and easy to go around. The Expression is a lot heavier and bigger. In case you've got a craft area or room to scrapbooking so you don't have to transfer it frequently, you get a lot more choices with this system.

Cricut Accessories For Scrapbooking

When in regards to a scrapbooking, the ideal accessories will make all of the difference. That is the reason it is a fantastic concept to select Circuit accessories to the scrapbook needs so you know that you're receiving quality scrapbooking items that you may depend on.

When you would like assistance with your scrapbooking, then Cricut is a title you can rely on to supply you with quality tools and accessories that will assist you make good scrapbooking. By way of instance, you may take your topics and thoughts and make them a reality in ways you wouldn't have been able to do before.

With that the Cricut cuts along with other accessories, so you could be as imaginative as you desire. If you do not believe you are a really artistic or creative individual, you may make use of these tools to produce things that you never would have been in a position to consider earlier. If you're creative, then you are able to take that imagination even further using all the resources which Cricut can provide for you.

You can make use of these resources to your benefit to make a number of the greatest scrapbooks about. Your thoughts can become a fact so it's going to be easier than ever before to capture those pictures and mementos coordinated into scrapbooks that you cherish forever.

When deciding upon those accessories, create a record of

the ones that you want and want the most. Then return in order beginning with the ones which you want the maximum and moving down into the ones that you'd like to have since you are able to afford it. Then you're able to buy these one or 2 at a time before your group is complete and you've got each the excellent Cricut accessories that you need on your scrapbook sets.

Here are merely a couple of those safest accessories out there:

- Deep Cut Blades
- Cricut Stamp Refill
- Cricut Jukebox
- Cricut Cartridge Storage Box
- Cricut Color Fashion
- Cricut Cutting Mats
- Cricut Spatula Tool

Now That you learn more about picking Cricut accessories such as scrapbooking, then you are able to apply this on your personal scrapbooking. You may discover that it makes your scrapbooking much simpler and it also provides you more layouts and more ways to utilize your imagination for exceptional scrapbooking.

Cricut Expression - Worth the Money

The Cricut Expression is selling like hot cakes on the web! What is all of the fuss about? Here I shall provide you a fast collection of the very best characteristics, and enable you to determine if the Cricut filler actually cuts !

- The Cricut Expression is a really sophisticated crafting device, compared to Cricut Create along with also the Cricut Personal Electronic Cutter. The very first thing strikes you is just how large this new version is, with regard to its dimensions.

- It's been fabricated by a group of seasoned specialists with the only purpose cutting letters, letters, and contours in appropriate sizes throughout the use of this 12 inches x 24 inches cutting mat.

- This superb electronic model may perform different kinds of paper clippings such as vellum and maybe even vinyl. Crafters can cut paper to little .25 inch bits, and around 12 inches x 24 inches.

- Different layouts with a vast assortment of contours can be drawn up via this complex device.

- It's packed with unique attributes like Plantin faculty publication font and Accent Critical type capsules, inclusive of this 12 x 12 mat for cutting functions.

- Cricut certainly made Expression with teachers and schools in your mind. This system could be popular set up in the course space, there is little doubt about this!

- The most recent model generates an impressively high number of distinct paper cuts. But, crafters considering forming dices measuring less than 51/2 inches may nevertheless elect for your Cricut.

- The most important drawback could be that many crafters discover that it's tricky to produce sufficient space for the setup of the outer machine, because of the bulky casing.

- In addition to the core attributes, you get welcome bonuses such as, Vehicle Load, Mix'n Match, Fit to Page, Flip and Fit to Style etc.. This updated model can be packed with all the Accent Cartridge that will surely develop the attribute of scrapbook designs.

- Together with the awesome Flip choice, you are able to track the image or chart changing its instructions. This is much more entertaining than it seems!

- The center point process is a real-time saver. It helps users to place the blade over the authentic center indicating of this photograph or picture, then trims the particular place on the photograph for you - really convenient.

- The multi-cut mechanism allows the unit to reduce thick sized chipboard considerably deeper than previously.

- The Line spin placing helps you to fix the blade into another line when performing heavy cuts.

- Additionally the Mat Size program will permit the user to place 12 inches x 24 inches or 12 inches x 12 inches.

Cricut Design Studio Help For Newbies - 5 minutes Tutorial!

Switch on your PC! If you have successfully set up on your Cricut Design Studio applications you need to observe the tiny green Cricut Bug appearing at you with large eyes directly out of your desktop computer.

When you load the program, you are going to be shown a huge window with elements that may appear odd (or not so odd) at first glance.

Here is a brief description of the chief things in the Cricut Design Studio applications to assist the newcomer (you!) Begin without yanking your hair to hair loss because the program's manual is a bit too lean:

1. the very first thing you'll see is that the digital mat that appears just like your bodily pad. That is your digital design area and where the majority of the action will occur. Begin by clicking on some other form in the keypad overlay (the major box only in addition to the mat) and play with the picture. You will see huge circles round the contour, these are known as"selection manages" plus they allow you to control and distort the picture in each direction.

2. The next thing you'll see is, as discussed in the past stage, the keypad overlay. This is the digital keypad which changes in line with the cartridges you have chosen. Each single time you click one the letters or shapes on it will show up on your digital mat so that you play it and layout exactly what you would like.

3. Third would be the two boxes only contrary to the keypad overlay: the chance library around the left and also the form properties box to your right.The chance library is precisely what its name implies, it is sort of an indicator of all of the cartridges out there. You are able to design to any of those cartridges and also utilize letters or shapes from various cartridges at precisely the exact same design but you will have the ability to cut just with all the cartridges you have (not trendy! ... I understand). The contour properties box allows you control the

selected letters or shapes with more accuracy. You're able to provide them X and Y coordinates (like back in college), you may give them exact height and width, it is possible to rotate themyou can nudge themweld them kern them.

What is nudging? Clicking the nudging switches moves the form you pick by very tiny increments. Use it if you have to make tiny alterations.

What is Welding? Welding allows you to have contours"glued" together if you cut them together with all the cricut. Simply make letters or shapes overlap in your style, when you flip the weld operate onto these overlapping letters will probably be glued together once you reduce them.

What is kerning? Kerning let's you define the distance between phrases. Utilize it to have a predetermined number (positive or negative) between phrases without needing to nudge them over and over again.

Matters To recall:

You can Layout along with all the cartridges which exist in the world (do not know for Other planets) however you can just cut together with all the ones that you've bought.

You May Use Other folks cut documents in case your not in a really creative mood. Just head Into the cricut message board or perform a fast search on Google to get "cricut layout studio trimming documents".

Make sure to upgrade your software if needed to become new cartridges packed in your cartridge library and to find bug fixes.

CONCLUSION

When in regards to arts and crafts, so you may never fail with Cricut Cartridges. In order to get many of years, lots of aspiring artists are inspired by different layouts and patterns offered by the capsules created by Cricut. Regular, a great deal of shops can market a small number of capsules because of growing demand of those products as soon as it comes to neighborhood shops. With the popularity of this line, a great deal of retailers also has been effective in leasing to your brand. For people that aren't into arts and crafts, then you might not understand a whole lot about Cricut capsules. But, we guarantee you that understanding more about those products can help yourself participate in more activities concerning paper crafts.

The finest thing concerning Cricut cartridges is that you don't ever appear to run out of ideas and choices. Whether you adore fonts, shapes or animation characters, you'll have the ability to locate a cartridge which can fit your taste. But when choosing a cartridge out of Cricut, the very first thing which you will need to take into account is how far your budget will probably be. The selection of costs of these capsules can appear as low as just a bit below fifty dollars, and may soar alongside a hundred bucks.

If you're the sort of person who enjoys a great deal of colors, you are able to stick with the fundamental silhouette cartridges and just take advantage of different colored papers to perform your cutouts. If you would rather create use of words, then state for the scrapbook designs, you might even use the ribbon cartridges. Additionally, there are people who are a massive fan of this certified character collection. You'll have the ability to use cutouts of your favorite cartoon characters from Disney and other animated movies. For many adults who have kids in your home, this is going to be a superb chance to bond with your kids and educate them how to generate their own art bits.

CROCHET FOR BEGINNERS

The Ultimate Step-By-Step Guide With Pictures
To Learn And Master Crocheting With Fantastic
Tips And Patterns To Do Beautiful Crochet Stitches
In One Day

Rachel Baker

INTRODUCTION

Crocheting is a common practice in the current world. It is a process by which a person creates fabrics through interconnecting loops of strands, threads or yarns of different materials. The complex process is made easier by use of a crochet hook. The name crochet hook has been derived from term crochet in the French language. This term is used to refer to a small hook in the French language. The term is also related to a German crock which means a hook. The crochet hook is made of different type of materials. These materials include plastics, woods or metal which are commercially manufactured and products made in workshops of artisans.

In order to clearly see the stitches while you are working, you will need a relatively big crochet hook. You will work with wool in the beginning, as it is the most suitable material to start with. Later, you will try cotton and other materials. Besides, wool is the material used for many projects. It is a good idea to master wool very well before trying something else.

To find the perfect crocket hook for your hand and your style may take some time. Now, as a beginner, do not think too much about it — finding hooks to make your work easier is enough. What you have to avoid is buying crocket hooks made out of plastic or bamboo because these are not easy to use. Bamboo ones are often inexpensive, made from natural material, and definitely cool. Plastic ones have wonderful color patterns. The problem is that the wool tends to get stuck on them and creates problems you do not need to have at your early stage. The best idea is to buy a plastic coated metal hook — not so fashionable, but easier to use for sure. Neutral and light colors are strongly suggested. Multi-color hooks can confuse you while you are crocheting.

Later, as you get more experienced and you start to use cotton too, metal crochet hooks are ideal. of course, you will build up a wonderful collection of every kind of crochet hooks with time.

For the best size for beginners, we have to consider that they differ depending on the country and the brand of hook. In the USA, the size that you need will be either a G6 or an H8 (better to have both) which is the European equivalent of 6 and 8. It is better to buy different sizes to start your new crochet experience. In this case, the advice of your favorite shop keeper will be very useful. The size depends on what you want to create. The size of the hook and the yarn you use determine the size of the item being crocheted. This is very similar to using various knitting needles. Thus, if you want a bigger square, you have to adjust the needle accordingly. Dimensions of the hooks become even more important if you want to use scrap wool and one is thicker than the rest. To get the stitches even, you just use a smaller sized hook for the thicker wool so that the stitches all look the same size.

Learning how to use patterns and graphs will fill your world with colorful, soft, fun, items you made yourself. Kids love the toys created with amigurumi and everyone loves a soft warm blanket. Learning to read and follow patterns and graphs will open up a world of beautiful items that you can make.

This explains and demystifies the art of reading patterns and graphs. Everyone is capable of reading them no matter how difficult it seems. Each stitch has a symbol or abbreviation and once you learn the symbol or abbreviation you can create finished items that others have taken the time to create.

Crochet is an embroidery method that utilizes a crochet hook with fiber or similar material. This fiber is most usually wool or crochet thread, but it could also be leather, rope, twine, or other inventive content.

Crochet fans are looking forward to finishing crochet creations that are usually useful, desirable, or helpful items in some way. Common initiatives typically involve Afghans, crocheted blankets, baby booties, sweaters, beanies, and squares of granny, shawls, pouches, tote bags, and many others. Several different things can be crocheted, including brooches, socks, and curtains.

It is also important to use different components in other

products to crochet. Crochet trims as well as edgings, for example, are common projects; you may add them to crocheted products, knitted items, as well as sewn pieces (including ready-made shop-bought items), such as purchasing some shoes, towels, and/or pillowcases, and applying a crocheted finish to each.

Crochet is a form of craft in which a small hooked needle or rod is used along with yarn to create items or sheets of fabric with different textures and appearance through using different techniques.

The main differences between crochet and knitting are the types of stitches and the techniques used. For instance, knitting incorporates using two same size needles at the same time to work the wool and create sheets of fabric at a time. With crochet, you only use a single needle at one time as well as your hands. This also means you only have one active stitch at a time, whereas in knitting you have many active stitches at any one time which can make it easier to accidentally drop a stitch without noticing.

Crochet is also remarkably easier to pick up over knitting; crochet has very simple beginner stitches which you can use even in the early stages of learning to create cute and funky little objects. It is a great encouragement for a beginner to see their hard work begin to grow and take shape in front of them.

CHAPTER 1
HISTORY OF CROCHET

No one knows when or how crochet has been made. It's because, instead of knitting, crochet was the artwork, rather than the advanced lace knitting produced for the Royalty and the upper class and eventually preserved for study in museums and historians.

Over the years, crochet has been more transparent than knitting needles and more flexible to make more fun and inventive clothing, shoes, Afghans and much more.

Historians assume that the lower classes invented Crochet.

It left someone who wanted luck in a sport and was evil. But when these textiles were made available to the new middle class, they were used mostly for knitting darn socks.

So, an informal crochet movement started with people who could find a few strands or threads and then made decorative knots and chains using their fingers. This initial attempt was probably similar to macramé instead of crochet but was still a cheap and revolutionary art for the masses.

The people of Turkey, Persia, North Africa, China and India may have started to make iron, bone, ivory and wood hooks around the 1300s. But before people began to "crochet in the air" as it was called in France in the 1800s there first evolved another type of knots and loops.

Since no one understood that the crochet stitch could produce a garment on its own, it turned to a technique known as' tambouring.' This method was first developed in China and includes crochet-like stitches created from textiles.

It was roughly 1700 that textile manufacturers stretched out a background material that was taught to frame and then passed the thread loop through the material using a crochet needle. The hook was combined into the first chain point when the thenloop was created.

By the mid1700s there were enough tambourine pieces from the East to inspire Europeans to practice the art of tambourine.

Finally, the fabric was removed and the first modern crochet was created using hooks made from silver, brass or steel by the Europeans, who learned to drum. Once upon a time, it was only the upper class who could crochet who inspired the masses to start drinking their socks and to dream of more imaginative outlets.

It was time, however, that people learned to make their hooks and to adorn their garments with the odds and ends of the fabric. (The crochets were used for the first time in Europe to create whole clothing and decorate existing clothing) The upper class, who made crochet fashionable, saw and proclaim it out of fashion, the growing middle class and its new crochet immediately.

Then the knits left, the lower classes couldn't afford, and just left to crochet until the queen Victoria took crochet and make it fashionable again.

Although in Italy and Spain, a more modern crochet version was born, the French developed the crochet in the late 1700s, naming it from the middle French word crochet or crochet knot. Throughout this time, crocheted lace was also made.

Later, standardized patterns that were easy to follow were circulated. At a time when standard needles were made, crochet in the middle of the 1800s became the most inexpensive way for the growing middle class to spend time on the fire and to make unique clothes, accessories and home decorations.

Modern crochet remains the needle-based art of people to this day. It is easy to understand, fun to do and much less restrictive than its knitting relatives.

I'm aware of a few, crochet types, the most commonly used, called, in the West, crochet, which involve a variety of methods, using, yarn and loop stitches; terms such as slip stitch, chain stitch, double crochet stitch, half and triple stitch and more.

Archeological findings suggest that Arabia could be the first place where a needle and hook worked cloth. Ancient findings from Egypt indicate skilled use of the needles and hooks from 950BC-1200BC.

Throughout its long history, crochet is a word from the French word "croc" which means "hook" and is believed to be employed by men and women.

A technique that can be used to sit, stand, lie or while in motion, use a variety of yarn, linen, cotton, silk and wool, including precious metal finely beaten and golden spun, with or without added beads or spangles, to manufacture garments, jewelry, bags, tapestries, tissue to cover furniture, make warm to light clothing, to similar crochet patterns found in India and North Africa demonstrate the hypothesis that crochet has been used in the Middle East for thousands of years.

Is it Tunisian crochet or is it Afghan or Tricot crochet?

Where and when the first surface appears like a cross between a hook and a needle.

Was it Tunisian? A crochet type that can look like crochet, knitting or weaving was the leading man of each of these fabrics?

Slip crochet stitch, maybe the earliest crochet and fabric type.

Broom-stick crochet is also known as peacock lace, where

and where did this come from?

Was it the founder of Europeans who traveled around the USA in covered wagons, had bulbs and hooks, got the expertise, brought them from their homeland, needed very warm bedding and clothing, began to create a fast and simple crochet style?

Irish crochet, traditional Irish crochet, 3D luxury lace characteristic of a net of picots (called fillers), ladies, romantic and beautiful, with its crocheted petals, flowers and leaves.

A subgroup called baby Irish crochet in Irish crochet is continuously working in squares or circular. In the 1870s, crochet was the salvation of many Irish families by making 12,000 to 20,000 crochet lace for their families during the years of the potato famine and beyond.

Bruges Crochet, a lace made in trebles and chain stitch, the crochet bands are combined to make a lace-like transparent string.

Bavarian Crochet, new to me, this regional crochet is something I need to know.

Aran crochet is like knitting Aran, it shapes a fabric with elevated areas coming from a flat backdrop.

Filet crochet was very common in the 1920s and 1950s and is famous due to the simple mesh structure and patterns in the lace, it's easy using Hairpin Crochet Charts, supposedly made in the Queen Victorian period by women using their hairpins and hooks to make a modern type of crochet that is used in linear and fine circular laces.

Today, we have replaced the pins with looms that are easily adjustable in size to make working this crochet shape easier.

Revival in the '60s as individuals began to make modern design garments by hand in non-compliant shapes and colors to the standards of the day.

Stripes, jacquards, patchwork, lace, fabric, hoops, knit, beaded, circles, rings, today scrumbling, crochet is a living art, reinvented and used in different and infinite ways using modern materials.

Ways that across history and the world have permitted people to fulfill their personal needs, earn money, feed their families, clothe themselves and their families, learn new things, and meet their needs.

Crochet in the early 21st century finds that its revival is new in manufacture, thousands of fashion and decorative products made, as well as in the hands of individuals who reveal old designs, designs new patterns and applications, handcrafted decorative objects, personal clothing and work of art.

Crochet styles are changing and Crochet is going to live on. A modern textile craftsman; work with beautiful materials; Australia Superfine Merino, Merino, Alpaca, Angora plus, Silks, Cashmere, acrylic, floating, beads; and wearable works.

Gayle Lorraine Designs by Gayle Lorraine Ancient techniques meet contemporary conceptions, East meets West, color, line, texture and balance which are important in fine art and sculpture, whether work is 1,2 or 3D.

Gayle paints on canvas and felt, wearable felt, Nuno, Calamari and Cobweb felt, yarns, buttons, Tunisian (Tricot, Afghani), crochet breadstick and a little Irish crochet, and a ton of simple crochet.

Annie Potter, a world traveler, and crochet expert said that crocheting started in the 16th century. Back then, it was called chain lace in England and crochet lace in France. In 1916, Guiana Indians' descendants were visited by Walter Edmund Roth. He found examples of crochet.

Lis Paludan, a writer and researcher from Denmark, had three theories. She said that crochet may have originated in Arabia then spread westwards to Spain and eastward to Tibet, eventually making its way to Mediterranean countries. She also said that crochet's earliest evidence was found in South America, in which a primitive tribe was claimed to have used crochet adornments during puberty rites. Her third theory states that early forms of crochet, particularly three-dimensional dolls, were found in China.

Paludan added that there isn't any convincing evidence as to how old crochet may be or where it really originated. It was not possible to look for evidence in Europe before the 1800s.

A lot of sources also claimed that crochet has already been known as far back as the 1500s. It was called nun's lace or nun's work in Italy because it was used by nuns for church textiles.

Another theory was that crochet was directly developed from Chinese needlework, which is an ancient form of embroidery known in India, Turkey, North Africa, and Persia and has reached Europe in the 1700s. It was actually called the tambourine, which came from tambour, the French word for drum.

In this method, a frame is used to stretch the background fabric while the working thread is held beneath it. A hook with a needle is inserted and a loop is drawn through the fabric. While the loop is still on the hook, the hook is inserted farther along with the fabric and another loop is drawn up to form a chain stitch. Tambour hooks are as thin as needles, which is why a very fine thread has to be used.

The Irish crochet was actually sort of a lifesaver for the Irish people. It delivered them out of the potato famine, which lasted for five years. They sold their crochet work to well-off people abroad. During this time, they had a hard time working and living. So, they crocheted in the day in between chores. When the sun has set, they use candlelight to see their crochet patterns.

However, keeping their crochet projects had been quite a

problem for most of them were living in squalor. They did not have a place to store their work. Keeping their crochet projects under their bed only made them dirty. Good thing, these things could be washed. However, most of the buyers from other countries were not aware that their delicate cuffs and collars were made in poor condition.

The Irish workers, including children, men, and women, were organized into cooperatives. They formed schools to teach individuals how to crochet. They also trained teachers and sent them to different parts of Ireland so they can teach more people how to crochet. Soon enough, the workers were able to design and create their own crochet patterns.

Even though a lot of people died in less than ten years, they were still able to survive the potato famine. More than one million Irish citizens perished, but many families were still able to make it through, thanks to their crochet projects. The money they made from selling crochet work allowed them to save up and immigrate to other countries. A lot of them actually went to America, taking their crocheting skills with them.

It was believed that two million Irish people went to America between 1845 and 1859 and four million more went there by 1900. The American women were busy with weaving, spinning, quilting, and knitting back then, but they were still influenced by the Irish to crochet. This explains why the Americans have also become adept at crocheting.

CHAPTER 2

HOW TO READ AND

UNDERSTAND CROCHET

Not all patterns are written out, or you might want to try your hand at working with patterns that aren't in English. While many American and British crochet patterns are written out like the one above, in Japan and other countries, crochet is typically charted. Instead of using words, these patterns use a pictorial chart. If you're a knitter, you're likely familiar with charted work; however, crochet charts are drawn out, rather than graphed.

Here, you'll see an example of a crochet chart. This chart creates a square like you might use to make an afghan. The numbers noted on the chart are row numbers, not stitch numbers; however, not all charts will include those.

Chart reading

Crochet charts are used for a variety of different projects and can, with a bit of practice, be more practical and effective than written instructions. Today, more designers are opting for charts or are including both charts and written instructions. For a complex chart, you may want to also use a row counter. A row counter allows you to click or move a bead to track how many rows you've completed. While this isn't typically necessary for a small chart like this one, it can be very helpful for larger charts.

Crocheting has been around for centuries. The term crochet originated from the words croche or croc, which is French for hook. It is relaxing, fun and simple enough that even beginners can learn it.

You only need two things to crochet: a ball of yarn or thread and a hook. All stitches are created by wrapping the thread or yarn around the hook. At first, you may find it a bit confusing or difficult to do. However, as you continue to do it, the entire process will be easier for you.

Most patterns begin with a series of loops, also called chains or a slip stitch. Nevertheless, you can easily learn how to create a foundation without using a standard chain. Projects are typically worked in rows wherein you have to switch back and forth. You can also stitch in rounds wherein you work around a ring of chains and create a geometric figure, such as a circle, hexagon or square. You can also use a motif or a geometric piece to stitch together and form your crochet project.

Crocheted Projects

In the early centuries, it was the men's job to create their own handiwork. Fishermen and hunters, for instance, created knotted strands of cords, strips of cloth, or woven fibers to snare birds or fish and trap animals. They also made fishing nets, knotted game bags, and cooking utensils. They created things that have practical uses.

Eventually, they expanded their handiwork to personal décors. They used these things during special occasions, such as celebrations, religious rites, marriages, and funerals. It was common to see ceremonial costumes that featured crochet-like ornamentation as well as decorative trimmings for the wrists, arms, and ankles.

During the 16th century, wealthy people and members of the royal family of Europe wore jackets, gowns, headpieces, and lace-trimmings. The poor people cannot afford such lavish clothing; hence, they used crochet to make their clothing more attractive. Crochet became their imitation of expensive lace.

Fast forward to the Victorian era, crochet patterns were made for birdcage covers, flower pot holders, card baskets, lampshades, lamp mats, tablecloths, wastepaper baskets, tobacco pouches, antimacassars, purses, caps, waistcoats, and rugs with foot warmers.

From 1900 until 1930, the women became busy crocheting slumber rugs, Afghans, traveling rugs, sleigh rugs, chaise lounge rugs, car rugs, coffee cozies, teapot cozies, hot water bottle covers, and cushions. During this time, potholders were popularized and became a staple in every repertoire.

During the 1960s until the 1970s, crochet became a free-form way of expression. This is evident in today's 3-dimensional sculptures, clothes, tapestries, and rugs that depict the realistic scenes and abstract designs of yesteryears.

Making fabric

Most of us when we think of crocheting we picture a nice lace shawl or something similar made from lace or yarn of some kind whether it be wool, acrylic or cotton. But these are not the only materials that you can use in crochet. Below are some other types of materials you can use to crochet that perhaps you have not considered until now.

Fabric Crochet is not a new technique; it has been around since at least the 1800s. There were actual rag rug patterns available in the 1910s, 20s, and 30s. The downside to working with fabrics is that it can be much more strenuous on your arms and fingers. It is easier to work with thread and wool but you will save money and do some refurbishing by doing fabric crochet. If you are someone that has a history of carpal tunnel syndrome then I would not suggest that you take up fabric crochet. Make sure that you allow yourself plenty of time to finish a fabric crochet project so you can well rest your hands between sessions of your project.

Pattern reading

You'll find stitch patterns written in two different ways. The first is the most typical and will be found in vintage patterns, as well as many modern American and British patterns. This is a fully written out stitch pattern, using typical and traditional stitch notation. Below, you'll find a list of common abbreviations, and a few notes about translation issues, as well as a sample pattern and a breakdown of what it means. Some modern designers in the west, as well as Japanese crochet patterns, do not rely upon written out notation, but on a graphic representation of crochet stitches. These look nothing at all like craft charts you might have used, like those for cross-stitching or knitting. They are, in fact, rather pictorial, with picture symbols written out for each round or row. Once you're used to reading crochet charts, you'll find you can do so with relative ease.

-Charts are much more commonly used for doilies or shawls, rather than simple projects, like a hat or afghan.

-Charts are rarely used for repeated stitch patterns but can be.

Written crochet patterns are still the most common in America and Britain. They are relatively easy to use, and pattern notation is largely standardized.

approx	approximately
beg	beginning
blo	back loop only
cc	contrast color
ch	chain
cl	cluster
cont	continue
dc	double crochet
dec	decrease
ea	each
gm	grams
gr	group
hdc	half double crochet
hk	hook
inc	increase
incl	including
lp	loop

mc	main color
pat	pattern
rem	remaining
rep	repeat
rnd(s)	round(s)
RS	right side
sc	single crochet
sl	slip
slst	slip stitch
sk	skip
sp	space
st(s)	stitch(es)
tog	together
tr / tc	triple (treble) crochet
WS	wrong side
yo	yarn over

Make a chain of any length desired, plus 3 stitches for turning.

-Row 1: Make 5 DC in the 3rd st from the end, * skip 2 ch, make 1 SC in thenstitch, skip 2 and make 5 DC in thenstitch *.

-Row 2. Ch. 3, and turn. Work 4 DC into SC * 1 SC into 3rd DC of previ-ous row, 5 DC into SC of the last row. Repeat from * across row.

-Repeat Row 2 to the desired length.

Let's take a longer look at this in a written-out form:

-Row 1: Make 5 double crochet stitches in the third stitch from the end of the chain. *Skip 2 chains, make one the crochet should be single the thenstitch, skip 2 chains and make 5 double crochet stitches in the thenstitch.*

-Row 2: Chain 3 and turn. Work 4 double crochet into single crochet. Work one the crochet should be single to 3rd double crochet of the last row, 5 double crochet into the single crochet of the last row. Repeat from * to end.

With just a little practice, the abbreviations will become second nature. You'll find them used throughout the patterns.

Do note: If you're an American and using a British pattern or you're British and using an American pattern, there's a bit of a quirk between the two languages.

British Notation	American Notation
double crochet (dc)	single crochet (sc)
half treble (htr)	half double crochet (hdc)
treble (tr)	double crochet (dc)
double treble (dtr)	treble (tr)
triple treble (trtr)	double treble (dtr)
miss	skip
tension	gauge
yarn over hook (yoh)	yarn over (yo)

Do you see the difference? The UK doesn't use the term single crochet; single crochet is called a double, and double crochet is called a treble. The treble crochet is called a double treble. Reviewing the pattern key can help you to know whether you're working with a British or American pattern, but it's an easy adjustment, especially as you get used to working the pattern.

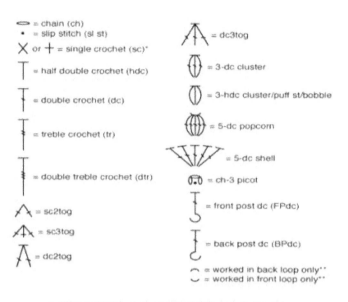

The key above illustrates crochet chart symbols. The symbols themselves are universal but do notice that the language refers to American crochet notation and work the stitches accordingly.

When assembled to form a chart, the symbols might look like:

You may notice something about this chart right away. It creates a visual very similar to the finished work, making it easy to realize what your project should look like, even if you don't have a picture of the finished work.

-Round 1: Ch 16, join with a sl st.

-Round 2: Ch 3, work one dc in the first chain of the last round. *work one dc in thenstitch, 2 dc in thearound* join with a sl st. (24)

-Round 3: Ch 3, sk 1 dc, sc in next, *ch 3, sk 1 dc, SC in next* join with a sl st.

-Round 4: Ch 3, *1 dc in first sc, sk 1 ch, *10 dc in 2nd ch stitch, sk 1 ch, 1 SC in sc* to last ch 3 loops. 9 dc in 2nd ch st, sl st to join to 3rd ch in initial ch 3.

-Round 5: Sc in 6th dc of last dc cluster, ch 5, dc in sc of prev round, ch5, *sc in 6th dc of the cluster, ch10, dc in sc of prev round, ch 5, dc in sc of prev round, ch5* join with sl st

-Round 6: Working backward to reverse direction, slip stitch in the first 5 ch stitches to the left of your hook. This returns you to the corner of your work. Ch 8, sc in the third ch of ch 5 of the last round. *Ch 5 sc in the third ch of ch 5 of the last round. Ch5, dc 3 in 6th ch of ch 10 of prev round, ch 3, dc3 in the same space*. On the last repeat, dc 2, using the first 3 chains of initial chain 8 to make the third dc. Join with sl st at the third chain.

-Round 7: Working backward again, sl st in first 5 stitches to reach the corner of your work. Ch 8, sc in the third ch of ch 5 of the last round. *Ch 5 sc in the third ch of ch 5 of the last round. Ch5, sc in the third ch of ch 5 of prev round, dc 3 in 6th ch of ch 10 of prev round, ch 3, dc3 in same space*. On the last repeat, dc 2, using the first 3 chains of initial chain 8 to make the third dc. Join with sl st at the third chain.

-Round 8: Working backward again, sl st in first 5 stitches

to reach the corner of your work. Ch 8, sc in the third ch of ch 5 of the last round. *Ch 5 sc in the third ch of ch 5 of the last round. Ch5, sc in the third ch of ch 5 of prev round, Ch5, sc in the third ch of ch 5 of prev round, dc 3 in 6th ch of ch 10 of prev round, ch 3, dc3 in same space*. On the last repeat, dc 2, using the first 3 chains of initial chain 8 to make the third dc. Join with sl st at a third chain.

(Note: Rounds 6, 7 and 8 are nearly identical, with the addition of one more ch5 loop per side in each round)

As you can see, that's a very cumbersome pattern written out. It's much easier to follow and understand working from a pictorial chart. This is the benefit of charts for complex and lacy work. If you'd like, you can even make your charts, either by hand or using online charting software.

CHAPTER 3
TYPES OF CROCHET

Amigurumi Crochet

This type of crochet is said to have originated from Japan. People would use this type of crochet when making toys that would be stuffed using this crochet. Ami means knitting or yarn that has been crocheted while amigurumi means a doll that has been stuffed. This type of crochet is therefore used when one is making these stuffed dolls through the use of heavy yarn. One can also make fan items and the large novelty cushions as well as the homewares.

Aran Crochet

This is a type of crochet that is normally ribbed and also one that is cabled. It is a traditional type of crochet which is made through interlocking cables. Through this type of crocheting, one can make sweaters and chunky beanies as well as scarves. This type of crocheting is said to produce very strong items as a result of the interlocking of the cables. This is the reason why people use it to make items that would need to be worn for longer periods of time. They can also be used to make blankets and aphgans as well as jackets and coats and also scarves.

Bavarian Crochet

This is a type of crochet which is said to work just like the granny squares, which were traditionally made. It is used when one wants to make very thick items and also when they want to blend in different colors when making them. This type of crochet is said to allow people to be able to blend in different colors without experiencing any challenges. They are able to do this by working on each part on its own. This helps them to be able to blend them together, which makes them come up with a very fancy item. The granny squares make it very appealing since one can even use squares of different colors. One can make blankets and shawls through the use of Bavarian crochet.

Bosnian Crochet

Bosnian crochet is used when one wants to make a dense and knit like material through the use of a crochet slip sew up. One has to, however, stitch different parts of a stitch on the current row. One has to ensure that the stitches are different in each row. They are able to achieve this through the use of the Bosnian crochet hooks, which are said to produce very good crochets. One can still work with the normal hooks; even the Bosnian hooks give better crochets than the other hooks.

This type of crochet is not very popular. This is because one would think that it is normal knitting when you look at the crochet. It is easy to work with it since the style used is easy to learn. People use it when one is making the scarves and beanies, as well as when crocheting items that do not require much time to be crocheted.

Bullion Crochet

This is a type of crochet that requires one to use a lot of time when making them. One uses many wraps of the yarn, which have to be put around a hook that is very long. By doing this, one is able to come up with a very unique stitch. This type of crochet is used when one needs to make the motifs and not when making crochets that require one to use the fabrics.

It takes a lot of time to produce the item you are making using this type of crochet since one has to be very keen when coming up with the patterns. The final product is normally very firm and thick, as well as stiff. A crocheter uses a method to make items that are meant to be long-lasting. One can make mats and stiff materials when they use this type of crocheting. This helps them to be able to come up with materials that are very unique and firm, so they can be used for a very long time without them wearing out.

Broomstick Crochet

This type of crochet is also called jiffy lace. It is normally made through the use of traditional crochet hooks. One forms make some stitches all round a very long as well as wide stick that looks like that one of a broomstick. In this modern age, people are said to use the large crochet hooks as well as the thick dowel when they are making the broomstick lace nowadays. It is a skill that people need to take their time to learn in order for them to come up with a well-made crochet. It is, however, a type of crochet that is said to produce crochets that are very beautiful and unique. One can make baby shawls using this type of crochet and also throw blankets that are normally used for the purposes of decoration.

Bruges Crochet

This is a type of crochet that is used when one wants to make Bruges laces, as the name suggests. One first creates ribbons meant for the crochet, which are sewed together in order for them to form the desired lace pattern. They are said to form very beautiful patterns that are also unique. This is because they are neatly sewed together. One can use different colors when making these patterns, which makes them even more beautiful. This type of crochet is used for making table mats and shawls as well as embellishments that are used for clothing.

Clothesline Crochet

This is a type of crochet which is said to utilize the stitches that were used traditionally. One uses a very thick yarn when making items using this type of crochet. They work on a rope that has to be very thick since when making mats, one requires something that will be so strong and which will be easy to style as well as shape. This type of crocheting is mostly used when one is making mats and baskets or anything that is required to be strong. One needs to have skills on how to make items using this type of crochet since they need to make first make the item they need to make on the ground before they can crochet it. This type of crochet is used in the making of mats and baskets as well as wall hangings.

Clones Lace Crochet

This type of crochet was said to be easy to make in the past and was very popular among people who love crocheting. It resembled the Irish lace, which was made because it was so easy to make. Clones knots are made, which makes as they are normally part of the crocheting process. One needs to learn this skill in order for them to ensure that they know how to make items using it. This type of crochet is used when one is making delicate dresses that require one to be very keen.

Cro-hook Crochet

With this type of crochet, one is required to use a hook that is double-sided in order for them to be able to achieve crochets that are double-sided. The crocheter is expected to work on an item from both sides. He or she can work from either side of the item, which enables them to come up with a very unique pattern. It is important for a crocheter to be able to learn this style before using it to male items in order for them to get good out of the outcome from it. One can make baby clothes and scarves as well as washcloths through this type of crocheting.

Filet Crochet

This crochet is a style that is achieved through the use of chains as well as double crochets. One achieves a crochet that has a pattern that is grid-like, which can be filled or left without filling. The space that is left is used in the creation of desired pictures which have to be included in the design. It creates patterns that are so unique and are neatly embedded within the crochet. This is something that is so unique about this type of crochet. All the squares that are left empty when crocheting may be filled with pictures of one desire. This type of crocheting is used when one is making the baby blankets, handbags, jackets, and kimonos, as well as when they are making cushions.

Finger Crochet

Finger crocheting is practiced when one barely uses the hook when crocheting. It is used when one is making some hand fabrics. During this type of crocheting, one will mostly use their hands to crochet. The patterns are fixed together to come up with one complete item. When one is making fabrics using this type of crochet, one cannot do it too fast. They will spend a lot of time crocheting, which may make them make very few items for a very long period of time. One can only make some string bags and small scarves which do not require much time when making them.

Freeform Crochet

When making this type of crochet, one does not create any pattern on the item. It is crochet that very artistic in nature and also very organic. Crocheters do not follow any plan, so one can come up with any kind of design that they would want. There are, however, people who do not like this type of crochet since they cannot do it without any kind of plan. They need to follow some instructions in order for them to be able to make their desired patterns. One can make art pieces using this type of crochet. They can design anything that they desire to design.

Hairpin Crochet

This is a type of crochet which is said to work just like the broomstick crochet even though in the past, people used crochet hooks. Pieces being crocheted were held together through the use of metals that were then. One is able to get very beautiful and unique crochets which are well finished. They are used when one is making shawls and wraps as well as scarves.

Micro Crochet

Micro crochet is used by the modern woman to make crochets. They make use of threads that are very fine and crochet hooks that are also very fine. A crocheter has to make sure that they are very careful when using the hooks in order to ensure that they use them in the right way in order for them to make the best types of crochets. They are used when one is making the talisman and embellishments as well as when making teeny tiny things.

Overly Crochet

Overly crochet is used when one wants to achieve an item that has stitches on top of the item, which enables them to be able to get a pattern that is raised. One can use more than one color when crocheting, which will enable them to be able to achieve unique and beautiful patterns. They can also make different designs using this type of crochet. One can use this type of crochet when making potholders as well as wall hangings as well as handbags.

Pineapple Crochet

When making items using this type of crochet, one does not follow any given pattern. This is because one can use just one general stitch, which they use to shape their desired patterns. One can use the pineapple when making these patterns. They use it to make scarves and shawls as well as wraps. This type of crochet is not complicated since anyone can learn it and be able to crochet items into their desired designs.

CHAPTER 4
TOOLS AND MATERIALS

Yarns

When you are beginning your crocheting journey, the first thing you will need, before doing anything, is to get all the supplies for your new hobby. There are a variety of different types of yarns and threads available for working in crochet. The vast variety includes options from alpaca yarn to banana silk and other alternative fibers. Some fibers are easier to work with, and some provide a nice texture to the project. It all depends on the handling which you will get from practice. The most common fibers used for beginners are wool, cotton, and acrylic. All of these have a lot of advantages and disadvantages as well.

Wool: This type of yarn is easy to reuse and unravel. Because of this property, if you make a mistake, it can easily be reversed. It's easier to work with, but working in the summer with this yarn becomes uncomfortable. In the summer, you might want to try out other lighter options.

Cotton: This type of yarn is also easy to use, but it doesn't easily unravel. If you are a beginner, working with cotton may seem a little harder than wool. It is less elastic than others. On the other hand, if your project requires that it maintains its shape, then cotton is better. It is lighter than wood so you can work with this in the summer.

Acrylic: When you are a beginner, you are making a lot of mistakes, and your projects are not coming out as you want them too. You're wasting a lot of yarn, which can be expensive if you are using other types. Acrylic is cheap, and it comes in a variety of colors. Its main disadvantage is that it's quite weak. There's a chance of breakage in acrylic, so you have to be careful when crocheting your project. If you are working with acrylic and your project breaking apart, then you should switch to other yarns that won't give you such misery.

Crochet Thread

All these types mentioned above are types of yarns but also use crochet threads as well. They are much finer and thinner. Because of this, it is harder to work with. If you're more interested in making light-weighted projects like lacy and open clothes, than starting from thread might be the option for you. Thread types come in cotton and acrylic.

People think it's difficult to work with thread, but that is not true. Here are some tips that can help you work with threads:

- As a beginner, user thicker size thread. Instead of using 30 to 20, use 3. Upgrade to those two sizes when you have developed your skills.

- Use a suitable hook according to your yarn size. A smaller number indicates a bigger hook, so doesn't get frustrated. The best one is the steel crochet hook.

- People get confused embroidery thread with crochet thread in buy that instead. Make sure you're buying a crochet thread.

- Draw your loops closer to the crochet head when working with crochet threads.

- To get good tension in your thread, hold the ends of the thread in your left hand.

Identifying yarn will become second nature to you once you get enough practice. After a while, you will be able to judge the type of yarn just by touching it. As a beginner, you will get all the information about the yarn on the yarn ball when you purchase it. It will have all the information that you need.

Additional tips

Yarn weight: One of the most important things to consider is the yarn weight. The sizes start from 1-7, with 1 being the thinnest and 7 being the thickest. If you are a beginner, then working with worsted weight yarn, which is number 3 yarn, is the best. It is of average thickness and provides you with enough grip.

Yarn color: when you are doing a big project, then, if you're using the same color, you have to buy a lot of yarn in that color. Don't make this decision by your eyes. Read the label on top of the yarn balls and match the color code between them. This will ensure that you have the same color.

Yarn texture: Avoid using extremely fancy yarns and stick to smooth yarns. Once you have developed the skill, you can move onto them.

Yarn price: Different fibers are available at different costs. It is smart to work with an inexpensive at first when you make a lot of mistakes. When comparing prices, people look out for yardage as well.

Crochet Hooks

To understand what hook will best suit you, you need to understand the parts of the hook first. It has three parts:

Head and throat: The hook at the end of the utensil is the head. Immediately beneath it, a shallow depression is formed, and because of it, it is called a throat. The throat guides the yarn inside the head. There are two types of head: tapered and inline. Tapered hook has a more rounded head, which does not seem in line with the rest of the body. Inline hook has a more pointed head, which does seem in line with the rest of the body. Whichever you choose, will depend on you. How to use both to understand which one suits you.

Shank

This is the part which denotes the size of the hook. The larger it is, the longer will the stitches you are making with it. It is right below the head and throat structure.

Handle and grip

To make you feel as comfortable as you can, your hook should have a nice grip and handle where you can rest your fingers. The grip is where you place your thumb, and the handle is where you place the rest of your fingers. If the grip is too long and bumpy, it will not feel comfortable, and you will have problem crocheting. A bad handle can cause pain in your wrists, which may progress over time.

Materials

It is important to note what kind of material the hook is made out of. It ranges from aluminum, plastic, glass, steel, etc. The hooks material depends upon the yarn you're working with. If you're working with a slippery yarn such as silk, it would be best to use a wooden hook instead of a glass or plastic so it might not slip easily.

What hook does?

As a beginner, you should start with a basic set of hooks. Other types are used for special pattern making and techniques, and it's better to not spend any penny on them until you have basic skills set into as second nature.

Basic hooks

You can buy these individually or in a set of different sizes. The set can be bought at any craft store or online. The sizes are denoted by numbers and/or letters. On average, hooks sizes range from about 5mm to 7.5mm. They are also mentioned as E-J, where E is the shortest, and J is the longest. It is better to buy it as a set rather than picking one individually. These hooks can help you complete your projects with ease if you are a beginner. Different weights of yarns use different length hooks.

Thread hook:

Crochet thread is a very thin and fine string that requires a hook that is also small. Thread crochet hook is smaller than other average hooks and often made out of steel so that it may retain its shape. If you are trying to work with thread crochet, then this hook should be your first choice. As a beginner, you shouldn't work with this yarn because it is difficult, but if you are, use this hook.

Ergonomic hooks:

They are made to provide maximum comfort to your hand. If you are suffering from any hand problems such as arthritis, then this hook is for you. Crochet is a tiring and time-consuming hobby, and if you feel uncomfortable, you will not do a good job. It reduces the pain and stress acting on your wrists.

Tunisian hooks:

Tunisian or afghan crochet hook is used in a specific type of crocheting called Tunisian crochet. It uses different stitching methods and also a different type of hook. It has two heads on each end of the hook.

Light up hooks:

There the same crochet hooks, but the difference is that they have a light in their head so that at night you can see where the stitch is going. This is for people who usually work at night and do not want to disturb their family.

Yarn Needles

They are a bigger version of regular sewing needles. It is mainly used for weaving at the end of the project. Like hooks, they have different sizes according to yarn's weight. They are mostly made of plastic, but other materials are available. There are a few differences between this and sewing needles:

They are a bit longer than regular sewing needles.

The yarn needles are dull and less sharp than sewing needles.

Mechanism of action is just like sewing needles, so if you

know how to sew, then you can work with them as well. They can be replaced by tapestry needles, which look very similar to them.

How to use them?

There are many ways you can use them

- At the end of the work, you will find that there are many ends of yarn left hanging on the side of your project. To get rid of them and secure your work, you need to weave them into place. This is done by using yarn needles.

- Granny square is a popular pattern design for crochet. Most of the time, you have to stitch them together by a mattress stitch or whip stitch. This is done by a yarn needle.

- It is used when joining dolls together or making other embellishments.

- When making surface stitches and decoration, you need this as well.

- Sometimes you get holes in your work, and you need to fix them. For repair, yarn needles play a major role.

Scissor

In crocheting, you will need a good pair of scissors to make a smooth working rhythm for yourself. Any type of sewing scissors will do the job if they are sharp enough and have not gone dull. To fulfill all your scissoring needs, it's better just buy a set containing scissors and perhaps some other accessories. Some sewing scissors are listed below:

Dressmaker shears: They look a bit bulky and have sharper cutting edges than normal scissors. The handle is shaped in a way that it is easy to cut cloth on a desk. It is mostly used by tailors and dressmakers hence the name. It is mainly used to cut fabric.

Pinking shears: It is the type of scissor which cuts in a zigzag pattern to give a certain design to the cut. It is used in scrapbooking and making cards. In sewing, it is used to make patterns and hemming. It should only be used on fabrics so that the blades do not get dull.

Office scissors: It is a traditional type of scissors that can be bought in any general store. Its blades match the handle. They don't have anything special to them. They can be used for cutting various items.

Embroidery scissors: They are small scissors that look like something out of a surgeon's box. They are used to make small snips and give a cleaner look to the finished project. It can also be used to cut ribbons and other materials.

Craft scissors: There look like any other general scissor, but it is mainly used for crafting projects. They don't get done quickly and last for a long time. They are available at any craft store.

CHAPTER 5
CROCHET PATTERN FOR
BEGINNERS

Slipknot

Knowing how to create the slip knot is the first step towards developing your crocheting ability. The slip knot is the basis of most crochet patterns, and therefore, you will need to properly master this so that you can build your ability to pick on other trends then.

So, you will begin with laying the thread on a flat surface, then looping once over itself. Here, you will have the tail yarn and working yarn. Tail yarn will be the part that is on the right side, while the working yarn is the end of the string on the left, which is pretty much how crochet begins. Then, loop over with your thread, so that the rear part if the wool comes over the one you are working with. Then, once you have done this, run the end of the wool over where they cross and move the loop beneath the working wool. After this, insert the crochet hook through the right side to the left, passing it over the wool you are working with then through the cross you have made. Then tighten the wool over the hoop. Pull lightly on both ends to tighten it. Congratulations, you've just made your first knot.

The Foundation Chain

This is the foundation chain, from which you then begin the crochet.

This is also called the chain stitch.

Here you hold the hook with the back end downwards while you hold the tail of the string on your other hand, using the finger grip that you are comfortable with using. Key is that you maintain it well such that it will be easy for you to make the loops without disrupting the movement of the crochet shaft.

Then move it over, with the wool coming to the left side of the hook, then move it to the left side of the first knot. Then, move working thread through the slip knot, and you will have one loop on the hook and another underneath it. This is your first chain.'

Do this over and over depending on the number of chains

that you want to create. So say you want to create twelve strings, then you will repeat this process over and over twelve times. Do this repeatedly until you can comfortably move the crochet through the working yarn, slip knot, and loops with ease and comfort.

Single Crochet (sc)

This comes to as the third step in making your crochet. Once you have your chain, you will have them looped into each other with v shapes, with the first end of it on the right side. Put your hook through the right side of the second v in the chain.

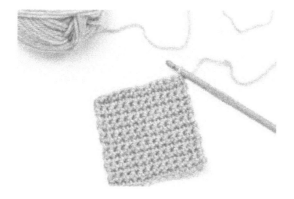

When you have done this, move over the working yarn, pulling it to the top side of the crochet hook.

Them move the working yarn through the V, bringing the moving wool through the procession you have woven, which will then create two running folds on the hook shaft. Then move it over once more, moving the working yarn back through the underside of the hook, passing it through the two loops you have when you do this. You will have one knot on the crochet hook. This is the first crochet that you have made.

To do this, you will need to understand that you will need always to be using the working yarn to make all the loops. That is why it is called the working yarn, after all. Be keen to keep it long then, as you do not want to run out of thread midway through your loop, bringing to a sad end the beautiful artistry that was taking shape.

Once you have completed your first single crochet, then repeat the process through each of the rows of the foundation chain and keep in mind that you will continue using the second V-shaped loops, as this will ensure that you do not have significant unsightly gaps in your knitting.

You will repeat this process for as long as you need, depending on the size of what you are knitting. Then, you move to a third party.

The Turning Chain

To begin with your turning chain, first you will need to flip over the foundation chain, but still maintaining the basic crochet rule - you work from right to left. When you flip it over, this will mean that you will have reversed it, with what was on the left now on the right and vice versa.

Then, begin to create a chain through the single crochet so that you create your first stitch.

Double Crochet (dc)

Here, you will yarn over then pull the hook into the fourth chain. Then pull through the string so that you now have three loops running through your hook. Then yarn over again and bring the hook through two of the circles, leaving the one at the end. So it again, and you have created one double crochet. You will then create three chains at the end to bring up a turning chain that will be the basis of the first double crochet in the new chain that you will form.

So, what patterns can you make from this?

DIY Scarves

Scarves are often rather straight forward when it comes to crochets, and you will find yourself making them rather quickly with the movements of that you have learned so that you do it

Efficiently and within a short time.

When you have finished with creating the foundation chain, you will then you will use the turning chai to create a long thin rectangle that you can keep knitting depending on how long and thus, how thick you want the scarf to be. As a beginner, this is a task that could take you a couple of hours a day, but you will be much satisfied with the outcome once you make it past the first couple of stitches.

Crochet Socks

Crochet socks are other easy designs that you will find it easier to so when you are a beginner.

According to Clara Parkes, the best yarns for socks are those that are elastic, meaning that they will need to stretch when you dip your foot into it, then wrap around the foot comfortably and warmly once you have worn it.

You will use your basic crochet techniques when you do

this, while you will need additional experience to make more complex socks like ankle-high socks and those with frilled edges or fancy patterns.

However, if you want simple, ankle-length socks, here you will need to alternate between the single crochet and double crochet. You will alternate between these two, lapping them over each other as you move through the foundations' chains, leaving the fabric closely-knit. This is what we call the seed stitch crochet.

So, you being with your foundation chain and then flip it over and begin to work on the turning chain, then make the first stitch, which will work as your first double crochet in the first row. Then, start to alternate between the dc and sc. Once you make your first dc, then, make the sc after that, then the dc, sc as you progress. Then make these stitches across the rows. When you start with a dc, you will then end the row with sc.

Once you finish, turn it over and begin working on the turning chain. But since you will have flipped over the wool, you will be working in reverse, your dc going above sc and your sc going above dc.

To continue creating the rows that you need, repeat the process from the moment when you made your first dc. You will repeat this process depending on how long you want the socks to be, though as a beginner, you should probably make it as short as possible as you work on your hand movements and ironing out the problems that may arise when you make a mistake.

Crochet Seat Covers

You will find these in many homes and cars, providing the room with an antique, authentic, and comforting feel. And the thing about these is that the patterns are relatively easy to follow, with the size and design also mainly depending on how you want it. But you will want to keep it straight if you're going to create an extensive material.

Once you have done your slip knot and created your foundation chain, then make four stitches and two rows. Then, in the first round, create eight single crochet stitches then make two sc stitches in each stitch.

In this, as with the socks, you will alternate between dc and sc. Once you create the two first rows, create another chain. Then, on the first row, the fourth chain from the hook, make dc through until the end of the row. Then, on the second chain, on the second row, make double crochet until then end. Repeat this on the third row, third chain. Once you have finished these, then close the terms. At this point, you will have a square granny design, and you will then work from here through with additional rows and chains depending on how long you want it to be and how much you want it to cover the seat.

However, if you want to add on color and make it larger, create additional rows and chains using wool from the color that you want to infuse to the cover.

Square Blanket

This is one other straightforward pattern that you can learn. This one will also turn out great with

Just one color, though you will then have to put a lot of time into it so that you can achieve the thickness and size that you want.

Using the basis of the granny square, make your foundation chain then create three more. Begin to make double crochets then, then loop them to create double stitches. After this, then connect these two double stitches through the third chain. After this, create another three dc but with the dc going into the foundation of the first round.

Go through this step until you get to the size that you desire. Or extra thickness, you could use the technique of socks and use alternating dc and sc to create additional loops and knots to the width that you desire.

Alternatively, you can still use this basis to create table cover, but then you will not need to make it substantial and thick as you would have with a blanket.

Crochet Sweater for Beginners

The basis of making the sweater is starting from how you would make the granny square. Make two of such rectangles, with the size depending on who you are making it. Use dc for making the rectangle that you will make the front so that it is one solid piece with minimal gaps. You could also

Use this for the back, or use sc to leave a see-through back for extra aesthetics.

So, create nine chains, with two rows. Here, make an "sc" through the second chain from the hook. Make a total of 8 sc. In the second row, stitch across the first chain, back loops only (blo). Then repeat this with the second row to row 65 or above, depending on the size to fit on waist, chest, and hips. Note that you will need the rows to be odd numbers.

Then move to the first row, and in the first chain, turn it and make sc across the band, with one running across each row, down to the number of rows that you have for the sweater and the region it fits. In the second row, loop through the third chain, turn and make double crochet across all rows. In the third row, repeat the second process. Through the fourth row through to the seventh, make the stitches on the chain lose.

CHAPTER 6
CHOOSING A CROCHET
PATTERN

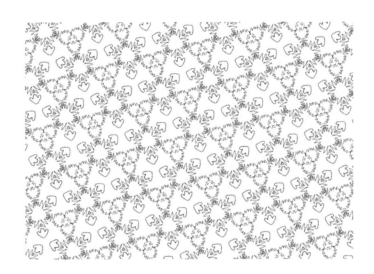

Basic emblem designs

Making crochet emblems is an extraordinary method to go through yarn scraps, and this was most likely the explanation they turned out to be so famous. You can sew emblems together to shape little things like sacks or pad covers, or to frame bigger things like tosses and infant covers. Joined emblems likewise make extraordinary scarves and shawls, particularly when made in gossamer mohair. Yet, if you are a learner, stick to less bristly yarns when making your first emblems since it is simpler to gain proficiency with the conventional afghan square crochet chart plain square method with a smooth, standard lightweight or medium-weight fleece yarn. When following charts, use hues as clarified in the composed instructions. The tones utilized in the outline are utilized to recognize the lines and don't show shading changes.

Try not to turn the emblems toward the finish of the rounds, however, work with the correct side continually confronting. Crochet instructions this square is worked in 4 hues (A, B, C, D), an alternate shading for each round. With A, chi 4 and get together with an ss to first chi to shape a ring. With A, chi 5, get together with an ss to third of 5 Ch. Affix off A. Cycle 2 With B, get together with an ss to a 2-ch corner.

Crochet flowers are enchanting even basic ones like these, which are altogether simple and extremely snappy to make. You might need to give them a shot immediately however wonder how to manage them. To start with, they make extraordinary pins, which, thusly, are immaculate blessings. Simply sew a self-locking pin to the back and possibly a catch or an artificial pearl to the flower focus. Sprinkled over a cushion spread, they will offer a strong expression in a room too. When following graphs, use hues as clarified in composed instructions. The image tones are utilized to recognize the lines and don't show shading changes. Join on new yarn hues as clarified. Try not to turn toward the finish of the rounds, however, work with the correct side of the flowers continually confronting.

Shell work scarf

This openwork scarf, using trim crochet frameworks and fine yarn, is warm anyway delicate enough to carry you from fall through to spring.

To crochet, the shell configuration used for this scarf, insert your guide into the single crochet join from the underneath. Work the twofold secures for the shell, see plan above, into the sc. Complete the shell by working 5 copies into a comparable Sc join. Desire the shell to "fan-out" inside the scarf by working an Sc into the accompanying chain space already working the accompanying shell gathering.

Color work

One-concealing crochet has its charms, yet using your inventive innovative brain to join shades is both testing and satisfying. The sum of the crochet color work techniques is definitely not hard to master and is worth experiment difficult various things to consolidate color work join structures, stripes, jacquard, and intarsia.

Jacquard and intarsia crochet are both worked in single crochet secures. Jacquard is commonly worked with only two tones in progression; the concealing not being utilized is passed on over the most noteworthy purpose of the underneath and attaches are worked over it. Exactly when a concealing is used extraordinarily in a zone of the crochet rather than over the entire segment, the intarsia strategy is required; a substitute length of yarn is used for each portion of concealing. Bobble stripe crochet instructions this example is worked in 3 hues (A, B, C). With A, make a difference of 2 chis, in addition to 1 extra. Work the accompanying columns in stripes, rehashing this stripe grouping—1-line A, 1-line B, 1-line C.

Column 1 (WS) 1 had in third chi from a snare, *skip thenchi, work (1 had, chi 1, 1hdc) all in thenchi; rep from * to last chi 2, skirt thenchi, 2 had in last chi, turn. Row 2 (RS) Ch 3 (considers first dc), 1 dc in first had, *chi 1, 1 bobble in then1-ch spa; rep from *, finishing with chi 1, work (you and embed snare in top of 2-ch at end of the column, you and draw a circle through, you and draw through first 2 circles on snare) twice all in the same spot (3 circles currently on snare), you and draw through every one of the 3 circles on a snare, turn.

Line 3 Ch 2 (considers first had), *work (1 had, chi 1, 1 had) all in then1-ch sp; rep from *, finishing with 1 had in the top of 3-ch, turn.

Column 4 Ch 3 (considers first dc), 1 bobble in then1-ch spa, *chi 1, 1 bobble in then1-ch spa; rep from *, finishing with 1 dc in top of 2-ch at the end, turn.

NOTE: bobble = (you and embed snare in specified set, you

and draw a circle through, you and draw through first 2 circles on snare) multiple times all in the same set (4 circles presently on snare), you and draw through every one of the 4 circles on the snare to finish 3-dc bobble.

Triangles spike fasten

Work concerning close shells as follows: Line 5 Ch 2 (considers first had), 1 had in the first dc, *work (1 had, chi 1, 1 had) all in then1-ch spa; rep from *, finishing with 2 had in the top of 3-ch at the end, turn. Rep columns 2–5 to shape pat, while proceeding with stripe grouping.

Crochet instructions NOTE: spike set = don't work into thenset, yet rather embed snare front to back through the top of set 1, 2 or 3 columns beneath this set, you and draw a circle through, extending the circle to the tallness of the line being worked (and encasing the skipped set), you and a draw through the two circles on the snare to finish a stretched sc. This example is worked in 2 hues (A, B). With A, make a numerous of 4 Ch.

Column 1 (RS) With A, 1 Sc in second chi from the snare, 1 Sc in every one of rem chi, turn.

Column 2 With A, chi 1 (doesn't consider a set), 1 Sc in every Sc to end, turn.

Columns 3 and 4 With A, (rep push 2) twice.

Column 5 (RS) With B, chi 1 (doesn't consider a set), 1 Sc in first Sc, *1 Sc in thenSc, 1 spike set in the top of Sc one line beneath thenSc, 1 spike set in top of Sc 2 lines underneath thenSc, 1 spike set in top of Sc 3 lines underneath thenSc; rep from * to last 2 Sc, 1 Sc in every one of last 2 Sc, turn.

Lines 6, 7, and 8 With B, (rep push 2) 3 times. Column 9 with A, rep push 5.

Rep columns 2–9 to shape pat, finishing with a pat push 5 or 9. With A, make the establishment Ch. At that point work in stripe pat, rehashing the accompanying stripe grouping line A, 1-line B, 1 column C.

Fundamental data Trouble LEVEL Intermediate SIZE 12 x 20in (30 x 50cm) YARN Any DK weight yarn will work for this undertaking CROCHET HOOK F/5 US (4mm) snare Ideas Yarn needle Measure 15 sets x 20 columns for every 4in (10cm) square Intarsia cushion this basic support cushion is worked in two pieces and has an appealing jewel and stripe intarsia design. The example incorporates the alternative for a twofold sided cushion or for crocheting one side in plain crochet.

NOTE When changing yarn shading: with yarn, an additional guide into thenset, get through a circle, change to yarn B and crochet the two circles on the snare. Work the following line in yarn B. Changing the yarn is finished in the final venture of the past join.

Unordinary yarns

On the off chance that you need to break the repetitiveness of working with fleece yarns, why not evaluate some irregular materials? String, wire, cloth strips, and plastic strips are loads of enjoyable to crochet with, and the materials utilized can be reused ones. To take you through the procedures in question, a speedy to-make thing appears with each of these "yarns." It isn't prudent to attempt to figure out how to crochet with uncommon yarns, so ensure you are deft at shaping single crochet fastens before endeavoring to work with them.

String crochet

Firmly crocheted string structures a tough texture appropriate for compartments. Since it is normally neither too thick nor excessively slender, garden twine is a decent decision for a first-string crochet venture. It is likewise simple to get and frames a texture that holds its shape well. Crocheting around the string holder utilizes a self-locking pin as the join marker select a snare size for your picked string that will shape a firm, tight single crochet texture. For instance, a size 7 US (4.5mm) crochet snare was utilized here with a characteristic nursery twine.

To evaluate string crochet, make a little round compartment. Start with cycle 1 of the flat hover instructions. Move marker up at end of each round keep on following the circle design, what's more, work adjusts 2 and 3. Work the lines as firmly as possible. If the crochet doesn't appear to be sufficiently tight, start again with a little snare size.

Edge framed by working into just back circles continues working rounds of the circle design until the circle is the ideal size for the base of the compartment. At that point to begin the sides of the compartment, work 1 Sc into the back circle just of the highest point of each join in the following round as appeared. This structures an edge. On all the rest of the rounds of the holder, work 1 Sc in each join of the past round, working through the two circles of the highest point of the join beneath in the standard way.

Wire crochet

For whatever length of time that it is fine enough, the wire is anything but difficult to crochet with, even though it takes a little practice to deliver even lines. Similarly, as with string crochet, it is ideal to adhere to straightforward single crochet for wire progressively intriguing lines are hard to recognize Crocheting a beaded wire bangle the least demanding wire thickness to crochet with is a 28 check (0.3mm) copper wire, which can be acquired online from creating stores or stores that sell gems supplies. For this wire size, you will require a size D-3 US (3mm) crochet snare. Among the twisting, vaporous wire circles. Adding globules to wire crochet is the most ideal approach to jazz it up and transform it into straightforward gems like the simple-to-make, flexible bangle that appeared here. String all the dabs onto the wire before you start crocheting with it. The bangle worked here utilizes around 27 glass dabs (6–7mm in distance across), however, it is in every case best to string on around 10 more than you might suspect you'll require if you have miscounted.

Make your outline for your dab adornments, demonstrating where the dots are to be set. This is the diagram utilized for the basic bangle. (How to function dot crochet.)

Utilizing the wire with the dots on it, make 8 chains to begin the highlighted bangle. At that point follow the diagram to work the beaded crochet, working the fastens freely.

At whatever point the situation of a globule is come to (consistently on an off-base sideline), work up to the last you of the join, at that point slide the dot up near the crochet and complete the fastening. End with a right-side (non-globule) push so an inappropriate side will look for the following line

CHAPTER 7
CROCHETING BACKGROUND

C rocheting fabrics are said to have been in existence since the earlier times. Its origin is however unclear since the skill was mostly been spread verbally between interested parties. They would copy the crochet pattern from someone's original work. This would result in different types of crochet mistakes hence no perfection of any of the styles.

Research states that crocheting may have started in china through their needlework which was a very common practice in Turkey and India as well as in North America. It is after this that the crocheting methods reached Europe but they would refer to it like a tambourine. Tambourine evolved to 'crocheting in the air' since the fabric used in the background had to be removed in order the stitch to stand on its own.

Crocheted fabrics became popular in Europe in the 19th century. Instructions about crocheting were first published in a magazine in the year 1823. The magazine had detailed information about the color plate which contained different styles. After publishing the magazine, the first crochet patterns were printed in 1824.

Mlle. Riego do la Branchardiere is said to have contributed

a lot in the popularity of crocheting in Europe. This is as a result of the patterns that she published in the 1800s which were so easy to duplicate. The pattern were given to millions of women who had an interest in crocheting. This was a sure way to ensure that the patterns reached as many women as possible whether they could.

Many women around the world started copying the patterns which made crocheting so popular. There are a lot of materials that one can learn from on the internet. One can, therefore, learn about crocheting from websites and different sites on the internet. Different crochet pattern have also published which contain different and unique crochet styles. It is therefore evident that crocheting has greatly evolved which has made it so popular. Many modern crocheted clothing is already being sold in our markets worldwide.

What makes one think of crocheting?

Many people around the world have mastered the art of crocheting. This is as a result of the many benefits that come with it. Different people will, however, crochet for different reasons. There are many people out there who may be wondering why people crochet. They do not see enough reason why one should spend their free time crocheting. Most times, they lack the motivation to start crocheting so it would be great if I highlight a few reasons for crocheting.

Crocheting is a stress reliever: Crocheting has been tried

and proven to be one of the activities that help people to relieve stress. This is because as you crochet, you can forget all the challenges you may be going through. All your concentration is on the pattern making so all your mind is occupied. As you crochet, all that is in your mind evaporates which helps a lot in relaxing your mind. Whenever one needs to learn a new crocheting skill, they have to go through different, sites and also apps which normally engage them mindfully. One forgets everything they are going through since they are curious to learn a new skill.

Crocheting brings a great sense of accomplishment: There is no better feeling than seeing people wear or cover themselves with items that you crocheted yourself. It makes you feel great about the time you spent crocheting the items. It isn't a waste of time as you can see them enjoy the fruits of your labor. That feeling is so fulfilling that you will want to keep crocheting. You will also keep on discovering new patterns and after implementing the skill, there will be a great sense of fulfilment.

Crocheting enables you to have an alert mind: People grow older each day. Crocheting offers a lasting solution to people who would want to remain alert as well as stimulated. One has to remain alert especially when they are working on new a new pattern. Isn't it, therefore, important to engage our mind with crocheting?

Keeping the tradition alive: We mostly inherit the

crocheting skills from our parents, aunts and even from our grandmothers. It would be a great thing to keep the tradition alive by passing it on to the people around us. It is very important to ensure that we pass down the crocheting art to our children and even people around us. For every crochet, there is some bit of love from the people we learn the art from.

Crocheting keeps you busy: Whenever one is crocheting, their mind is fully engaged. This means that they are busy hence will not be thinking about anything else. Being busy is beneficial in that, one won't be idling around without doing any meaningful thing. For most people, crocheting is a hobby so they use their free time doing it.

Enhancing one's creativity: We learn a new trick every day. Through crocheting, one can perfect their skills by designing new patterns. They can creatively mix different color schemes to come up with beautiful patterns which make the crochets to be more appealing. It is through Crocheting that one can experience a comforting effect from the great textures created through the repeated movements using yarns of different colors.

Health benefit: Apart from relieving stress, crocheting is of great benefit to people suffering from arthritis. This is because as one works through various stitches, the fingers remain nimble hence reduce the risks of arthritis. People who get Alzheimer's attacks are also advised to consider The Economic part of Crocheting

Many people around the world have been able to learn crocheting skill. It is an industry that has grown and has empowered very many men and women around the world. This has greatly improved the economy. Below are some of the economic impacts of crocheting. Do crotchets have an economic impact? Several people may not find crocheting beneficial. They may not see it as a source of income, but it contributes immensely to the economy.

During cold seasons people look for warm things to keep them warm. They, therefore, have to purchase scarfs, sweaters, socks and other products made from yarn. This increases the rate of yarn production as a result of the increase in demand for crocheted items. This is said to lead to the growth of the economy. Below are some of the economic impacts brought by crocheting.

So many crocheting companies have been opened which has created employment opportunities for many families around the world. They can take care of their families from the income they earn from the crocheting companies.

Women can crochet items and sell them to people in their neighbourhood which enables them to earn some income. This helps to improve the economy since they do not become dependent on the government for their survival. The government is, therefore, able to concentrate on other development projects since its people are not overly dependent on them.

People have also been able to come up with unique patterns and have published them in which are sold to interested parties. This acts as a source of income for the publisher which also helps in the growth of the economy.

The experts in this area have also taken up the role of training more people in crocheting. This ensures the empowerment of more people which means more skilled individuals in a country.

Individuals who have specialized in information technology also develop apps which contain crochet instructions. This has helped people to have easy access to the skills so anyone can install the app and learn the skills in their own free time.

Social and Traditional Impact of Crocheting

Crocheting has had a great impact on our society. The skill keeps on being passed on from one generation to another. This has helped a lot in impacting of people's lives socially and even traditionally. Below are some social and traditional impacts brought about by crocheting?

For Charity: Most often, we find ourselves with different types of crotchets which we mostly make during our free time. One can craft some items and give them out for charities. It will always feel great when one benefits from an item crocheted with a lot of love. It will act as a way of showing your generosity and sense of care for others. One will feel good when someone appreciates something that was made purposely to suit their need.

Aesthetic value: Crocheting can display the beauty of a tradition. Before the invention of big companies that dealt with the manufacturing of clothes, people used to wear crocheted clothes. Some people make crochets to beautify the environment. One, therefore, makes items that they are sure that they will make their environment calm. This will enable them to feel relaxed whenever they are around.

Boost self-esteem: We all feel good when complimented for doing something so well. Compliments motivate us to produce better crochets which are better the lastones. When we sell the crafts we made or give it as a gift, it boosts your self-esteem. You feel great about your accomplishments. Self-esteem can also be built through learning new skills. One can feel productive which creates beauty through self-expression.

Reduces stress and anxiety: We all get stressed up at some point in our life. We may become anxious as a result of the strenuous activities we may have engaged in on our daily activities. One needs to give themselves a break. Getting a yarn and crochet would be of great help in relaxing their mind. It is through the repetition of the stitches as you count the rows that your mind gets some kind of relaxation. All the anxiety thoughts are set free since your focus is on creatively making the crochets.

216

Eases and relieves depression: Our emotions keep changing depending on the occasion. For instance, in the grieving period, it seems impossible to overcome your grief. Most times we feel like the world has come to an end. Crocheting can be a comforter during the grieving period. Crafting such as crocheting is said to be helpful in the stimulation of dopamine which enables one to feel happier and emotionally stable.

Keeps one busy: Imagine you are left at home alone. No other work for you, you can choose to do some crocheting. You will be relaxing at the same time keeping yourself busy. You don't have to create wonderful products out of it. The whole idea is to keep your mind engaged through a useful course which may help you earn some income or even contribute to charity. In a scenario where you are following up on a program on the television, your hands will be busy crafting while your eyes are glued to the television. The best thing about crocheting is that one can engage every member of the family. They will be able to contribute to various ideas about what you are making and suggestions on colors and even designs.

Brings communities together: There are many ways to bring people together. One of them is having yarn crafting introduced to a community. They can have a meet up in public to do crocheting. The organizers can organize a fiber fair together with related events. This will be of great help since people from different places will be able to meet and share ideas. They will be able to learn from one another hence more creative designs. The community can even come together and build yarn stores which will benefit the community from the sales made in the store. All the participants can also buy the yarn at a reduced price which will enable them to make more crocheted items for sale. They in return become more productive which brings economic empowerment amongst them.

CHAPTER 8
TIPS AND TRICKS

10 Tips to get you started

1. Learn all you can about crochet supplies so you can purchase what suits you.

2. Remove all obstacles in your way. This can be your long hair, jewelry and cats (because they cannot resist a ball of yarn!) so you aren't interrupted while you work.

3. Position the yarn in a place that unwinds easily.

4. Be prepared to switch hooks. Novice crocheters often work too tight or too loose. If this is the case for you, change your hook. (Too tight = a larger hook needed, too loose = a smaller hook needed).

5. Take the time to make gauge switches, practicing all the stitches that you'll need for a pattern.

6. Don't be afraid to experiment to make a project your own. If you make a mistake, you can always unravel the last few stitches.

7. Take a break. If you get frustrated, taking a breather can help you refocus when you come back to work.

8. A break is also good for hand and finger stretching. You don't want to injure yourself as you work, or you might never get to finish your project.

9. Keep up to date with everything crochet. There are plenty of online e-zines and forums filled with all of the latest patterns, tips, tricks and information. You never know what you'll learn!

10. Of course, the best way to master crochet is through practice. After all, practice makes perfect!

Left-Handed Crocheting

Being left-handed needn't stop you learning to crochet. It may seem challenging at first, after all most patterns are aimed at right-handed users, and attempting to manage these will have you working backwards. Below are a few ways to get around this:

1. Reverse the pattern so that you're holding the crochet hook in your right hand. This means that the 'wrong side' of the pattern is actually 'the right side'.

2. Practice holding the hook until you're comfortable. A lot of left-handed crocheters have created their own variation on the 'pencil' or 'knife' hold, into a way that suits them.

3. Learn by sitting across from someone right –handed, mirroring their movements!

Tips in Creating Your Own Pattern

You may get to a stage where you have been crocheting for a while, and you'd like to try your hand at creating your own pattern.

To do this, there are a few things you should keep in mind:

• Master all the basic crochet stitches before you start, so you know the appearance and usage of each one.

• Follow a variety of patterns, noticing the mechanics of how they put a project together.

• Learn to count stitches and rows, so you'll be able to work them into your own.

• Experiment as much as you can with materials, tools and ideas.

• Get decorative with your creations. Practice with shapes and styles.

• Try to modify an existing pattern for practice.

• Learn how a gauge works – it's a great way to calculate stitches effectively.

• Sketch what you'd like to create to assist you in the shapes you'll need.

• Start simple and small, building complexity as you get used to it.

• Write everything down as you go, and maybe allow other crocheters to practice your pattern to get a better idea of how it'll work.

Crocheting in the front loop only

Novices to crocheting are bound to make this mistake. This is why we couldn't stress enough the importance of learning how to place the hook inside the stitch, as this represents the foundation of this handicraft. This mistake is likely to happen especially if the hook tends to slip from time to time and you don't realize this right away.

How do you avoid this common mistake? What you have to do is simply have a closer look at the detailing of each row as you work. Basically, you should analyze each row. While this may seem tedious and time-consuming, if you practice enough, you'll get the hang of it and you won't have to do it any longer. In time, your stitches will become second nature to you, so you won't have to stress about it.

Your work seems to be getting wider and wider

This is likely to happen to anyone – beginners and advanced crocheting fans as well. Therefore, you shouldn't feel too discouraged if it seems to happen to you. This is bound to occur when you're not paying close attention to the stitches. On that note, one way to avoid this from happening is by counting your stitches – in this way, you will prevent ending up with more stitches than you had in mind when you first started working on this project.

You might be doubling up into one stitch or, without your willing, you might end up working a stitch in a turning chain. The safest and simplest way to prevent this from happening over and over again is by counting your stitches. To that end, you might count each row as you finish, or keep an eye on the shape of your project, and determine whether it is developing as you had in mind.

You might feel that this is time-consuming, but believe us, it is more time-consuming to realize that you've been working for hours in a row to realize that you've made a mistake and you have to do the entire thing all over again.

Not focusing on counting the rows while working

This mistake also has to do with maximizing your time. The same way in which it is advisable to count the stitches to the project you're doing, you should also count the rows to avoid unwanted mistakes. When you're crocheting, you can easily get distracted, as your mind tends to wander off, especially if you're watching a tv series or anything of the kind.

Staying focused is essential if you're just starting out, so make sure you are there, in the present, when working on your project. Otherwise, you'll realize that there are five extra rows of crochet and you have lost your valuable time. You might resort to utilizing a row counter in case you end up doing the same mistake over and over again, as it will come in handy.

Creating Your Own Pattern

You may get to a stage where you have been crocheting for a while, and you'd like to try your hand at creating your own pattern.

To do this, there are a few things you should keep in mind:

• Master all the basic crochet stitches before you start, so you know the appearance and usage of each one.

• Follow a variety of patterns, noticing the mechanics of how they put a project together.

• Learn to count stitches and rows, so you'll be able to work them into your own.

• Experiment as much as you can with materials, tools and ideas.

• Get decorative with your creations. Practice with shapes and styles.

• Try to modify an existing pattern for practice.

• Learn how a gauge works – it's a great way to calculate stitches effectively.

• Sketch what you'd like to create to assist you in the shapes you'll need.

• Start simple and small, building complexity as you get used to it.

• Write everything down as you go, and maybe allow other

crocheters to practice your pattern to get a better idea of how it'll work.

How to Hold the Hook when Crocheting

It is very important that the hook is held properly while doing crochet work. This will reduce the incidence of pain in your wrist and will even make your work go on smoothly. There are two major methods mentioned in crochet literature. They are the pencil hold and the knife hold.

- The pencil hold: One way of gripping you hook is by holding it with your thumb, index finger, and middle finger. You can just imitate the way you'll hold your writing pencil.

- The pencil hold

- The knife hold: You can also hold it like your knife, with your palm on the handle, your three fingers wrapped around it and your index finger pointing towards the head of the hook. (See illustration)

The Knife hold

Which of the two methods mentioned above is better?

In the real sense, we all have different ways of handling stuff. We all hold our writing pencils differently, and it is part of what accounts for the differences in handwriting. Two different people might also have different ways of holding the knife. So, I will say find the style that suits you and crochet away!

Right and Wrong Sides of A Crochet Piece

In the art of crochet, working at the wrong side might lead the crocheter into making errors and therefore result in frogging. Working on the wrong side can also give a crochet result that is entirely different from what the crocheter had in mind (or in the picture.)

How do you avoid working on the wrong side of a crochet piece?

You can avoid this by not doing any crochet on the tail of the yarn. The tail of the yarn is the length of the yarn between your piece and the ball or skein of yarn.

For the piece to be on the right side, the tail should be at the bottom right corner.

CHAPTER 9
MISTAKES TO AVOID

Mistake 1: Putting Pens

P lace pens look like such a headache. Significant and also dangly ones get in your way. Tiny ones might not glide smoothly on big needles. They all take some time to put on the needles and also add an added action to relocate them while weaving stitches. After that, why utilize them? They form a pointer while you knit.

From simple garter stitch to difficult shoelace, stitch pens advise a knitter that some kind of various requirement needs to happen. When switching over to a different yarn, a brand-new stitch, or a pattern repeat, a marker states, "Hey, take note here."

When first learning to knit, starting knitters get lost in the methods, the stitches, the feel of the yarn, and more. Utilizing a pen provides a beginner knitter back to the facts, back to considering the pattern to determine what comes next, even directly back to putting those last couple of stitches in to develop a beautiful boundary.

When I initially learned to knit, I made the common mistake of not making use of pens. I assumed that as long as I adhered to the pattern, every little thing would work out great. Well, it didn't. If the design called for the same kind of stitch in the pattern, however, various one for the boundary, I occasionally kept knitting the pattern stitch to the end of the row.

My mistakes didn't show up until I weaved a whole lot more rows. As I had not yet found out how to undo stitches without removing rows, I needed to choose between eliminating several rows or leaving the mistake in the item. In some circumstances, I did not find the errors until impeding the piece far too late after that.

How to Fix It Correctly

If the pattern does not call for putting pens, there is no reason you shouldn't work without them. Try putting pens at the start or end of pattern repeats, right after or right before a border side, at a sign up with when knitting in the round, or at a color modification for Fair Isle knitting. All good options as well as up to you to select which ones work best for you.

If you fail to remember to add a marker while knitting a row, you can include a pen by using a marker pen, which is available to move over the needle. Additional alternative needles are running a small item of thread between the stitches and over the needle. Make a knot in the loop. On the following row slip the thread as you would certainly with a metal or plastic pen or replace it with one of those.

For a task with a lot of rows, stich markers function similarly well for counting rows. Utilize a piece of contrasting cotton yarn or a yarn that won't leave little bits and also parts of fiber behind when gotten rid of. Take a tiny part, connect a knot as well as slip it over your needle before completion of a row. Knit a set variety of rows, such as 5 or 10, and add another marker. Clip out when all set for ending your completed job.

If you neglect to add one of these little markers, thread a needle with cotton yarn and also carefully run it via a stitch. Make a knot in the string, and you have one more pen. The pens that open and close make a great additional option for keeping track of rows. These could be included while knitting the row or after.

Mistake 2: Picking the incorrect Cast-On

Externally, every cast-on does the same thing by creating loops on a needle that get dropped off by drawing yarn through them with a 2nd needle. However, a standard knitting error made by several beginners can be to choose the incorrect cast-on for a task or to alter the cast-on recommended by the pattern developer.

Each type of cast-on has a function beyond developing those first loops. A cast-on sets the phase for the garment. For instance, when casting-on stitches for the leg opening of a sock, the wrong cast-on can make it a fight to get the sock on over your foot or worse, it can trigger the top to fall around

230

your ankles.

Cast-on either offers the edge of your job both stretch as well as elasticity or just sufficient stretch for putting it on while sustaining the continuing to be stitched in the garment. When you make use of an elastic cast-on, such as a weaved cast-on, the edge of your project will relocate conveniently.

Nonetheless, if you utilize this type of cast-on for something like the neck of a gown that you wish to lie level, it may not support the stitches in the corset, causing it to gap open rather than stay flat against your skin.

The Fix

If a pattern does not state which cast-on to use, numerous knowledgeable knitters use the long-tail cast-on as their go-to cast-on. Moderately stretchy with a tip of the framework, the long tail-cast on help a lot of jobs

If the cast-on looks too limited, removing and beginning again with a various one may be your most beautiful. Believe me. I've done this more frequently than I like to confess, but obtaining the cast-on right makes the rest of the project job far better.

If the builder selected a particular cast-on, however, your cast-on side features too much overall flexibility, try out casting-on with an inferior sized needle, proceed to the needle required in the pattern to start your very first row. Alternatively, if the cast-on has excessive structure, cast-on with a bigger sized needle, then move to the appropriate size for the very first row.

If the job has way too much elasticity at the cast-on edge, usage progressed, finishing methods to add definition to the side.

Mistake 3: Binding Off Too Tightly

The tension utilized when binding off helps give form to your job. When you bind off stitches as well snugly, some facts take place.

It makes obstructing your process to the perfect measurements harder, normally impossible since a restricted bind off squeezes your stitches towards the biggest part of the job.

Your cast-on for a toe-up sock might be excellent, however, if you bind off the leg opening tightly, good luck getting that sock over your ankle joint. The same fact occurs for neck or wrist openings.

It makes an inflexible straight side that doesn't feel or look good, which frequently contrasts with the soft qualities of the rest of the job.

If you commonly knit with tighter stress, move your stitches to a needle 1 to 2 dimensions larger than used for the job. Bind off with the larger sized needles.

If you typically maintain tension by wrapping the working yarn around your fingers while knitting, drop it for the bind off. Instead, freely drape the working yarn over one finger or between 2 fingers for taking in the stitch. Allow the yarn to move over or between your fingers to stay clear of the extra stress.

If you knit within the American or United Kingdom style, keep the yarn in the middle of your fingers, as well as wrap it freely around the needle to make the bind off stitch without drawing it as tight as you would certainly for a typical knit or purl stitch.

Most significantly, inspect the tension after the last bind off stitch as well as before you reduced the yarn. If it also looks tight, meticulously unpick the stitches, putting the stitches back on a needle, and redo the bind off. Yes, I've done this too.

Mistake 4: Selecting the Wrong Yarn for a Project

Whether knitting from your very own design or from a pattern created by somebody else, choosing the right yarn for the task helps ensure the garment turns out lovely.

In some cases, you do intend to see if a dimension 80 tatting cotton thread knits just like gossamer Shetland. And that's a high point to do since testing when knitting creates enjoyable times.

Nevertheless, using the right yarn does have an objective and also recognizing exactly how different threads drape, lose, knit-up, tablet, and more make a distinction. Besides, yarn weight and color contribute to the yarn option.

When a coat pattern requires a DK weight merino wool, as well as you pick a fingering weight alpaca, not only will the gauge be off, but the sleeves, as well as sweater, will pool at your wrists as well as middle part respectively because alpaca's soft fibers drape higher than wool. Possibly you desire that appearance, yet if not, why waste the initiative?

Changing the fiber also impacts the garment. The majority of pet fibers have a halo, with mohair and angora revealing the most halo. These fuzzy tendrils of the texture add extra warmth to a weaved garment. When selecting them for a shoelace task, the halo hides a lot of the pattern.

Garments that are required to stretch, such as for example gloves in addition to socks, won't take just as much if knitted with materials, such as for example silk or bamboo. When using dark tinted yarns, stitches become low-key or shed, especially when knitting lace or any pattern with twisted stitches.

The Fix

When selecting yarn not asked for in a pattern, check out the yarn tag. Reference the yarn weight and the producer's suggested needle dimension If it suits the pattern's yarn weight and needle sizing, and when the yarn coincides or identical fiber, from then on, the thread must operate within the project.

When weaving lace and you intend to use fiber that creates a halo, select a pattern with an even more open job. The stitches will undoubtedly be extra defined with a mild misty radiance from the halo rather than getting shed in all that fuzz.

Furthermore, when knitting shoelace, select lighter tinted threads if you desire the shoelace layout to be a prominent attribute. When utilizing dark-colored yarns, the adverse room of the open holes ends up being a noticeable feature. Pick which style you wish to see in the completed garment.

If you wish to use silk yarn when the pattern asks for wool, you must rework the gauge and view the stitch tension. Without woolen's elasticity, silk yarn knits-up with even more structure as well as less bounce, which implies a garment might have a tighter fit.

Mistake 5: Starting a Project without Swatching

The scourge of lots of a knitter's existence, a swatch makes lots of points for knitters of any experience level. It shows if the yarn you've picked helps the job. It shows if you are knitting to assess, which suggests if you'll have sufficient yarn to finish the task, and also if you require to readjust for sizing. It likewise shows the pattern, which lets you understand if you have selected an excellent yarn color.

Various other advantages of Swatching consist of:

Learning if the dyer established the dye appropriately (If they did not, the color would run when you dampen the swatch for obstructing)

Enquiring if the pattern, as well as yarn, blocks well

Learning if you like the pattern to determine if you need to proceed with the task

The Fix

Make a swatch per the pattern directions if the pattern doesn't consist of a swatch size; after that, select one that's four times as big as the gauge. For example, if the design asks for four stitches to 1 inch over four rows, after that knit a swatch that has at the very least 16 stitches, as well as 16 rows.

The added stitches and rows give you more to obstruct and also will show you just how the item looks.

CHAPTER 10

CROCHETING TECHNIQUES

Increasing

Increasing is used to add more stitches to a row, this can be helpful when you want your work to grow in size. If used the right way, increasing can also create a beautiful design.

Increasing is very simple to do; you simply add more crochet stitches, that is all there is to it! You are not limited to putting one crochet stitch per chain. You can create a variety of shapes and sizes simply by adding maybe 1-2 extra stitches per chain.

To begin you can either start with just a chain or even a panel of fabric. The following example uses a small square of crocheted fabric. Start off with a normal single crochet, now instead of moving on to the then stitch, put your crochet hook back into the same stitch again as shown:

Pull through another loop and add another single crochet, you now have added 2 single crochets into one space:

Increasing is as simple as that, you can stick to just increasing at the very end of your rows or you can increase in every stitch along.

You also don't need to have just 2 single crochets in each stitch either; there are a number of very attractive stitches available to you which involve putting up to 10 single crochets in a single stitch. Doing this can create a wonderful fan or shell effect in your work.

Decreasing

The process of decreasing means that the number of stitches you have per row goes down, this technique is used for shrinking down your projects or tightening edges.

As mentioned in the increasing, you are not limited to how many decreases you can have in a row. If you want just to decrease at the ends of a row then you can but if you want to decrease in every stitch along then by all means go ahead!

The only limitation you have when decreasing is that to decrease you need 2 spaces, this means you need two stitches to do it, so if you have an uneven number of stitches in your row then 1 stitch needs to be a regular stitch.

Decreasing is a little bit more complicated than increasing as you are not just missing out stitches; there is a certain technique you have to use for your project not to have holes where stitches are missing; this method is referred to as crocheting two together.

Every crochet stitch has its own way of decreasing; however, this tutorial will cover how to do a basic single crochet decrease stitch.

To begin, insert your hook into the stitch and pull the yarn through as if you are going to do a single crochet this should leave you with two loops on your hook:

Now insert your hook into your thenstitch, do not remove or do anything with the two loops already on the hook. Once again hook the yarn and pull it through as if you were going to do a single crochet, you should now have a total of three loops on your hook.

Now wrap your hook around the yarn one last time and draw it through all 3 loops that are on your hook. You should now be left with one loop on your hook. This method shrinks 2 stitches down to 1. You can now either continue crocheting normally or perform another decreasing stitch:

Working in Different Loops

So by this point you should be able to do the most basic of crochet stitches such as slip stitches and single crochet. This covers how you can change the way you work looks by altering the location of your hook.

Below is what a single crochet stitch looks like from the top:

Here you can see that there is two different loops side by side that make up a single crochet. When you do a normal single crochet on top if this one, your hook goes underneath both of these loops; however you can crochet into those individual loops themselves, these are known as the front and back loops.

To work in the front loop only, insert your crochet hook through the first loop only, you can do any stitch you would like such as a single crochet.

FRONT LOOP

BACK LOOP

To work in the back loop, insert your hook through the back loop only; once again you can do any stitch you like at this point

Working in the front and back loops can make your work have an interesting texture and appearance. They can also be used to make the fabric fall or curve a certain way. It is typically used in patterns such as slippers or baby shoes to make them curve and fold in the right places.

Make sure to play around with the techniques mentioned, it will not only improve your understanding of crochet patterns but also broaden your knowledge of different things you can do with crocheting.

CONCLUSION

Crocheting will allow you to do a lot, from small bags to jackets and sweaters. There are various options available. Crochet pattern publishers also search for pattern testers. Contact several organizations and propose patterns for analysis.

Crochet patterns issued to the most competitively priced and excellent quality Chinese manufacturers. Lists can lead you to key information, such as the business size, main items, target audience, contact information, certifications and more.

Crotchetier does not confine him solely to the pattern instructions. It is necessary to make a personal decision which will improve the appearance of the project.

This guide is especially useful for those new to the hobby, but even the experienced expert can take advantage of crochet patterns. Crocheting will allow you to do a lot from small bags to jackets and sweaters.

There are various options available. Crochet pattern publishers also search for pattern testers. Crochet patterns offered by the most affordable rates and excellent quality Chinese manufacturers.

There are several more modern pattern printed, and in addition to traditional knitting lessons most yarn stores now sell crochet lessons. Filet crochet, Tunisian crochet, sprouts, sprouts and Irish crochet are all variations of the traditional crochet process.

These magazines most often have basic crochet patterns for beginners and even crocheters. Expert Crotchetier who crochet the designs mostly featured in craft magazines for a long time.

Anyone who crochets will tell you that a number of beautiful and completely original pieces can be crafted and made with their own two hands. For beginners, it brings with it a pleasure that was previously unknown to complete the first blanket, first scarf and first table cover.

And giving away crochet Christmas stocks is just one of the many wonderful crochet ideas. All crochet projects start with a knot of slip. Place the end of the yarn over the palm of your hand from right to left and back, and cross over your palm and put it again over the end of the first yarn string.

Expert crochet artist who created patterns for a long time mostly featured in craft magazines. Place the yarn over the crochet hook, thread it and pull back in the lastloop.

The specific design or style required for your decorating arrangement may not always be commercially available, but with crocheted accents of windows, you can always find a pattern that works or can easily be adapted with some creativity.

A vast number of free and commercial crochet patterns covering a wide variety of uses are available. Changes in fashion mean that various types of crocheted items are common in different eras.

Without comprehensive preparation and more freeform techniques, bead crochet bags could be made. The success of knitted and crocheted pieces persisted until the beginning of 1900s.

Whether you're searching for the Halloween costume or a holiday table runner, you can also get free samples of crochet patterns from art magazines, crochet, and libraries. The Internet, however, seems to be the viable alternative, since all of your free patterns can be accomplished by sitting in comfort at home.

This GUIDE is useful for those new to the hobby, but even the experienced expert can take advantage of crochet patterns. Some say it's a good idea to keep your things organized and stored in a crochet or knitting bag. But probably you can wait till your supplies and collection gets really going.

Start Crocheting Now!!